The Enigma of the Hour

AF760965

100 Years of Psychoanalytic Thought

Edited by Simon Moretti
& Goshka Macuga

Koenig Books, London

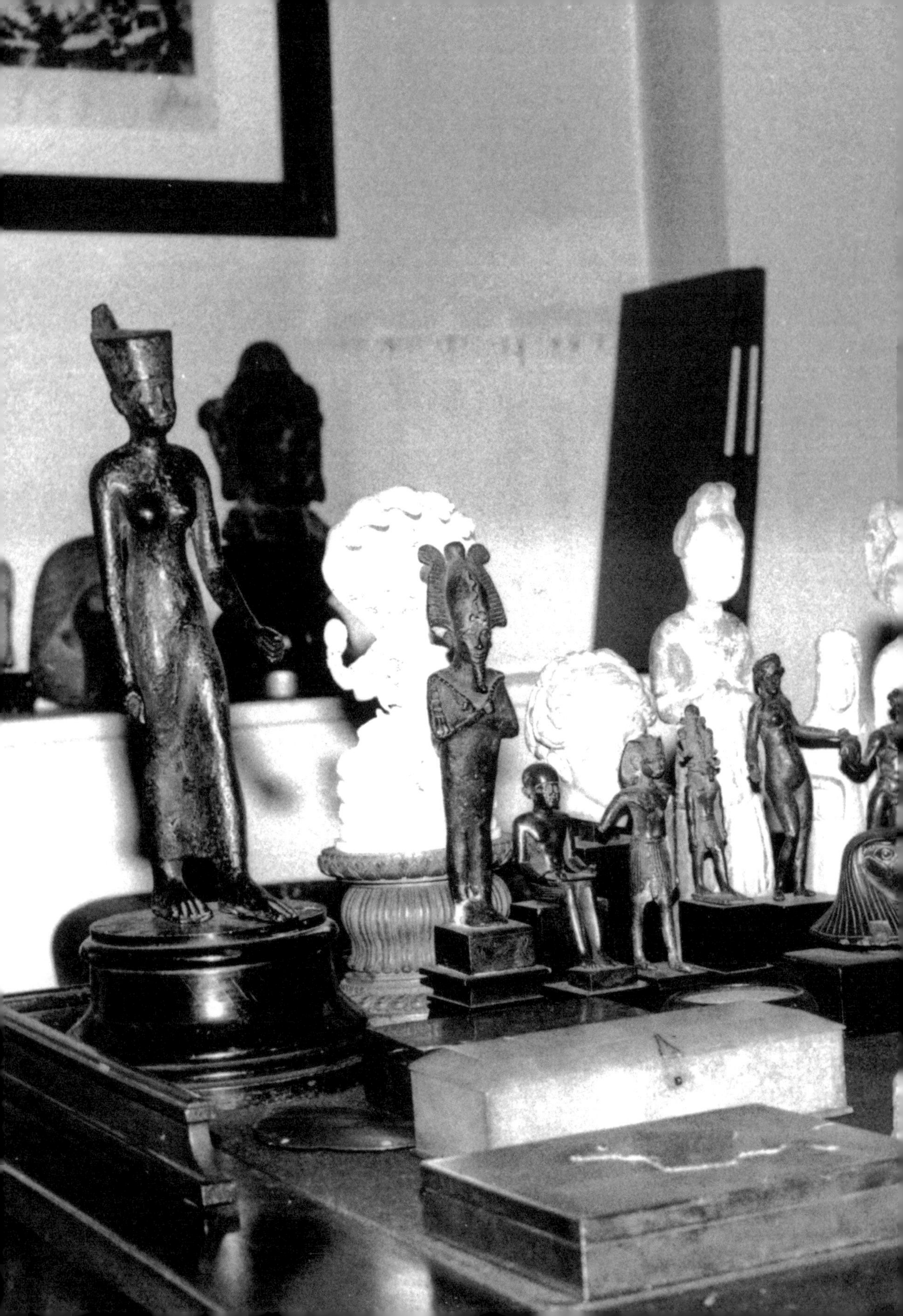

fig. 1

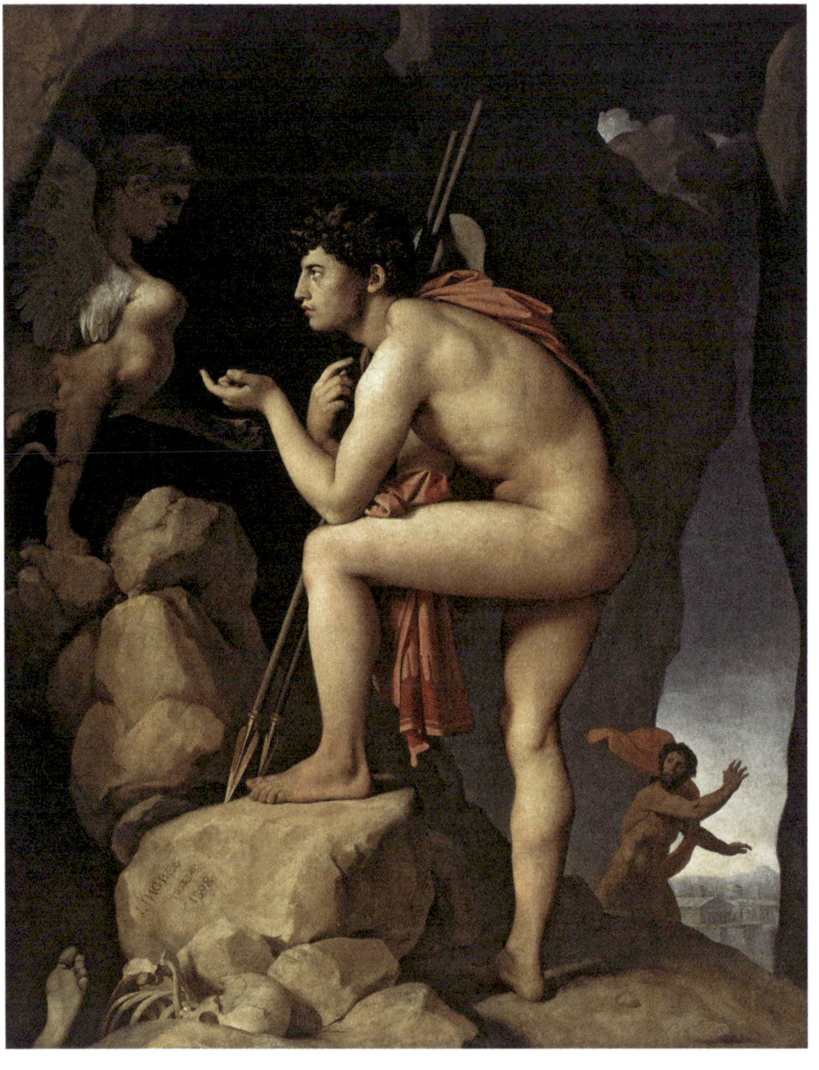

And, as imagination bodies forth
The forms of things unknown, the poet's pen
Turns them to shapes, and gives to airy nothing
A local habitation and a name
– Shakespeare, *A Midsummer Night's Dream*[1]

The publication in 1900 of Freud's 'On the Interpretation of Dreams' inaugurated the twentieth century in ways that could not have been imagined at the time.[2] Launched by his *magnum opus*, the explosive growth of the understanding of the human psyche would parallel equally explosive developments in the arts, which demolished existing ideas about the limits of representation – indeed, ideas of art itself. Tremors of this aesthetic revolution, felt in Turner's expressionist landscapes, were amplified by Cézanne's daring experimentation with form and colour, which was in turn elaborated by the Fauves and Symbolists. It was Picasso who, at the dawn of the twentieth century, radically deconstructed figuration, heralding the abstraction that dispensed with the figure altogether.

Remarkably, Freud and Picasso came of age as dominating cultural forces at the same time. Freud's exploration of the unconscious and Picasso's exploration of visual expression worked hand in hand to promote the flowering of Surrealism, and, a few decades later, Abstract Expressionism – movements that made explicit their intention to plumb and visually translate previously unseen, unknown parts of the mind.

Pandora's box had opened. While much energy has since been dedicated to vain attempts to stuff Freud's body of work back inside that box, nothing could restrain the myriad transformation of modern art, which rapidly expanded to include performance, conceptual, sound and video art; mixed media and installation; and sound and other ephemeral art, all of which emerged in the twentieth century. Absorbing and interpreting art-historical tradition art while witnessing and responding to the developments and devastations of our own time, artists continue to try to make sense of ourselves and our world: to 'give shape to forms unknown.'

So, too, do psychoanalysts continue to try to make sense of things – of ourselves, of course, but also of the art we make. *The Engima of the Hour: 100 Years of Psychoanalytic Thought*, curated by Simon Moretti with Goshka Macuga and Dana Birksted-Breen, commemorates the centenary of the *International Journal of Psychoanalysis* (*IJP*), which since its inception has published more than seventy papers on visual art and artists, aesthetics, and creativity. Looking back at the tangled, enigmatic marriage of art and psychoanalysis, it explores both its beginnings and its more recent incarnations.

Outlined in *The Interpretation of Dreams* is one of the foundational achievements that arose from Freud's self-analysis: his first, so-called 'topographical' model of the mind, a schema wherein unconscious forbidden or otherwise transgressive psychic material is kept separate and apart from the conscious mind by a psychic 'censor,' which determines whether, and under what conditions, unconscious material can pass into conscious awareness. He derived this model from the analysis of his dreams: working backwards, he traced the chains of associative links that led from remembered dreams to newly conscious wishes, fears, and fantasies. Freud theorized that this material was able to pass the censor and into conscious awareness by virtue of the disguise afforded by the transformative operations he called the 'dreamwork.' Like myth, dreams 'give shape to forms unknown.'

So, too, can art capture and distill dimensions of thought that 'remain unknown,' and elude linguistic formulation, as suggested

1 Shakespeare, *A Midsummer Night's Dream*, Act 5, Scene 1.

2 Sigmund Freud, *The Interpretation of Dreams*, Standard Edition, 4:ix-627 (1900).

fig.2

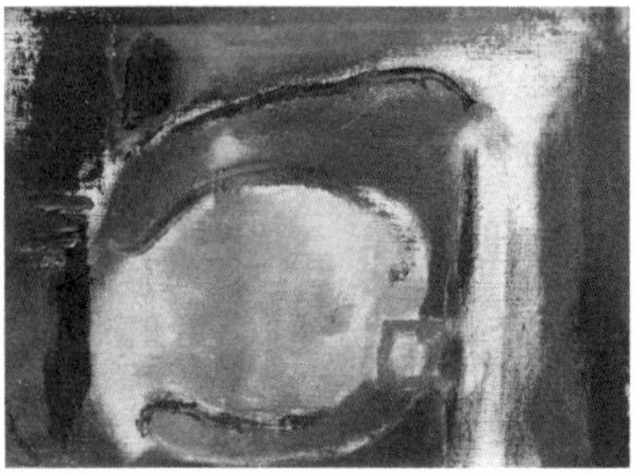

by the title of the single work in the exhibition by an artist who is also a psychoanalyst: Marion Milner's *A Thought Too Big for Its Concept*. Yet at the same time, the *non-finito* quality of the canvas reflects the impossibility of complete expression: at best, art remains a poetic evocation. It could be said that psychoanalysis anticipated the evolution of visual abstraction, from its initial stress on the articulation of the unconscious, to more contemporary emphases on felt, rather than thought experience, that 'airy nothing' that resists naming. It is precisely this quality that distinguishes Milner's contributions to the psychoanalytic literature, many of which concern creativity and its inhibitions.

Not unsurprisingly, much of *The Engima of the Hour* revolves on art that represents the mythical figure of Oedipus. In his dream book Freud describes how, during his self-analysis, his familiarity with classical myth allowed him to identify with Oedipus, who was fated to unknowingly kill his father and marry his mother. Freud's particular genius was to go beyond the personal relevance of the Oedipus myth, and propose that it narrativizes a conflict that is universal, rather than unique, what he (albeit in hetero-normative terms) called the Oedipus complex: the child's desire for the opposite-sex parent, which in turn generates a rivalrous, even (at least in fantasy) homicidal envy of the same-sex parent. Today, the conspicuous ubiquity of acknowledged Oedipal themes in Western culture makes it easy to overlook the fact that the second crucial theoretical advance generated by Freud's self-analysis, the Oedipus complex, was in fact inspired by and constructed around a work of art.

Freud extended this insight to other literary works, theorizing that Shakespeare's Hamlet was unable to avenge the murder of his father, the King, by his uncle Claudius because of his own guilt, having wished to do the very thing that Claudius actually did – namely, murder his father and marry his mother. In serial acts of translation – from myth to self, from personal to general, from literature to psyche and back to literature – psychoanalytic theory revolutionized not only psychology, but also literary, and later art criticism. If dreams were Freud's entrée to the transformations of the psyche, myth was his entrée to the transformations of art. His process was translation; his method, association. Thusly knit together are themes emerging from the constellation of art, objects, and archival material that *The Engima of the Hour* brings together and houses, aptly enough, in the Freud Museum: 'transformation; translation; association.'

fig.3

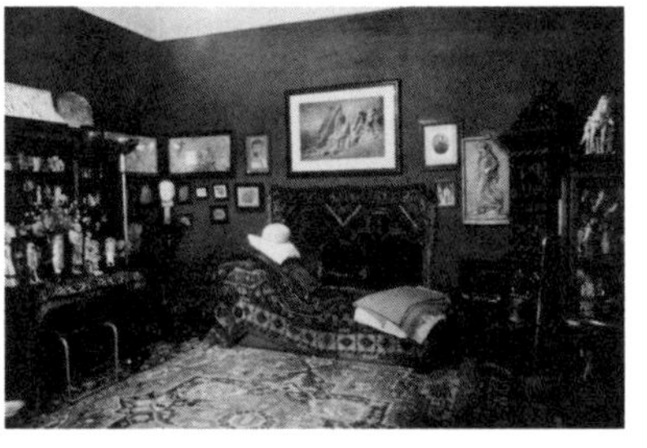

Well represented in the exhibition is the large collection of relics of antiquity with which Freud surrounded himself at home and at work, and which reflect his enduring fascination with ancient cultures and the mythic narratives that survive to define them. His sustained investment in actual physical artifacts, as well as the paintings and photographs that have continued to reinterpret mythic narratives, is wholly consistent with his tendency to rely on concrete visual analogies, including topography, architectural components,[3] and the layered depths of archaeological excavations –

3 See Diane O'Donoghue, *On dangerous ground: Freud's visual cultures of the unconscious* (London: Bloomsbury, 2018); Adele Tutter, 'Design as dream and self-representation: Philip Johnson and the Glass House of Atreus,' *Journal of the American Psychoanalytic Association*, 59:509–548 (2011).

the last of which serves, for Simon Moretti, as a metaphor.

In myth, Oedipus rescued Thebes and won its widowed Queen by solving the riddle posed by the Sphinx, the monster that terrorized the city since its King was slain. The Sphinx, a chimeric creature with the

fig.4

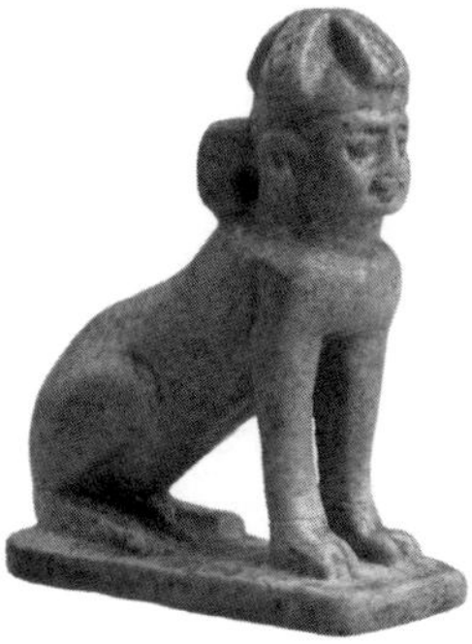

head of a woman, the body of a lion (and, sometimes, the wings of a bird) asks Oedipus: who first walks on four legs, then on two, and finally on three? Oedipus correctly answers 'man,' who, first crawls on all fours, then walks upright, and leans in old age on a cane. Oedipus and the Sphinx are thus forever associated with a riddle that condenses the transformations of human development, as marked by the locomotoric signposts of infancy, maturity, and infirmity.

fig.5

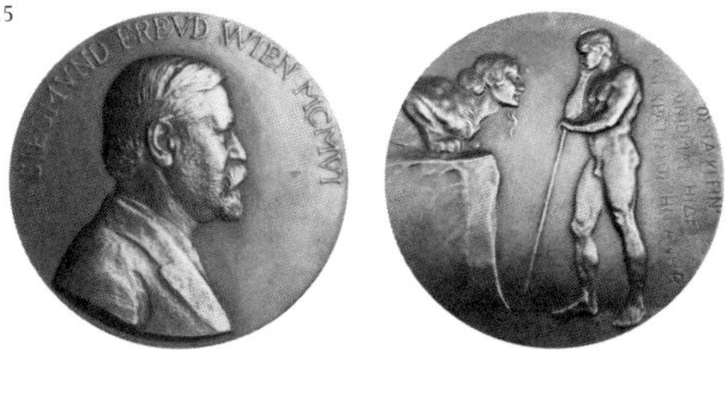

As psychoanalysis grew into a discipline, Freud's admiring colleagues came to see him as a modern day Oedipus – who in plumbing the mysteries of the human psyche had, like Oedipus, also solved the 'riddle of man.' The commemorative medal that in 1906 they awarded their hero on the occasion of his 50th birthday makes quite explicit this idealizing association: it bears on its obverse a dignified profile relief of Freud, and, on its reverse, an image of Oedipus and the Sphinx, accompanied by an inscription from Sophocles' *Oedipus Tyrannus*:

> ΟΣ ΤΑ ΚΛΕΙΝ' ΑΙΝΙΓΜΑΤ' 'ΗΙΔΗ
> ΚΑΙ ΚΡΑΤΙΣΤΟΣ 'ΗΝ ΑΝΗΡ
> *He who solved the famous riddle and was the most powerful man.*

Freud 'paled' after he was presented with the medal; he then disclosed that as a young student at the University of Vienna he used to stroll around the great Court inspecting the busts of former famous professors of the institution. He then had the phantasy, not merely of seeing his own bust there in the futures … but of it actually being inscribed with the identical words he now saw on the medallion.[4]

Aside from this felicitous achievement of a "dream come true" – which handily enough also served to dramatize Freud's belief that dreams represent a form of wish-fulfillment – other factors likely contributed to his dramatic response to the medal. One is the actual inscription, in which the Greek 'Λ' in *ΚΛΕΙΝ* (famous) was for unclear reasons replaced with the Roman 'L,' resulting in the misspelled *KLEIN*, which in German means 'small'. Freud might well have interpreted this mistake as a meaningful misreading, akin to the errors, jokes, and the now famous "Freudian" slips of the tongue to which he had very recently applied his dream-interpretative methodology – and, if so, this would have indicated to him that at least one of his colleagues (if they had indeed created the misspelling) felt (at least unconsciously) that Freud had solved a 'small' riddle, rather than a famous one.[5]

4 Thomas Mattonet, 'And Freud paleds … Cultural psychoanalytic reflections on a birthday present,' *Psyche – Z Psychoanal*, 56:1227-41 (2002), p.15.

5 See Sigmund Freud, *The psychopathology of everyday life: Forgetting, slips of the tongue, bungled actions, superstitions and errors*, Standard Edition, 6:vii-296 (1901); *Jokes and their relation to the unconscious*, Standard Edition, 8:1-247 (1905).

I had been interested in Freud's writing about parapraxis. Coincidentally, even before this exhibition became concrete, I had started a new series of neon text pieces based on my misreadings.

I like the idea that in these new texts, somewhere between a found text and its newly transformed and translated version mediated by the unconscious, a deeper truth lies.

I was already familiar with the Freud Museum and of course Freud's study and I had a vision of seeing my neon text work in that room. – Simon Moretti

fig.6

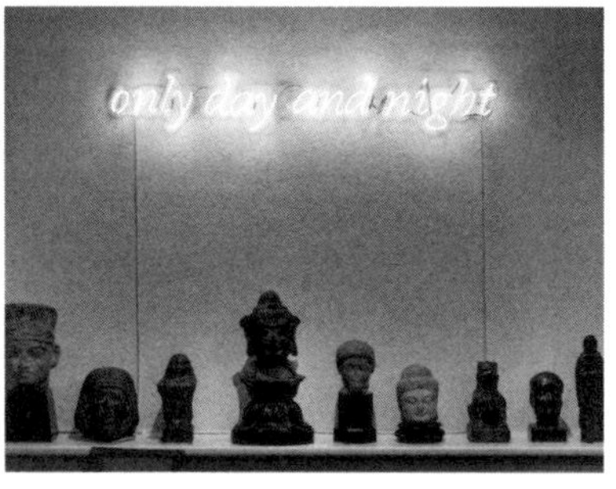

Freud soon realized that unconscious psychic content could be not only legible within the disguise of a dream or misreading, but also articulated by association: inferred from the temporal or spatial proximity of seemingly unrelated thoughts – reading between the lines, so to speak. Collage affords an aesthetic corollary of the derivation of unconscious meaning via the association of disparate elements; in the early twentieth century, the juxtaposition of different images and representations was perfectly suited to the still relatively new medium of photography. Inspired by psychoanalysis, Surrealism fully exploited the particular qualities of collage as it explicitly set out to visualize the unconscious.

Collage is represented in *The Enigma of the Hour* by several contemporary works. Demonstrating the enduring centrality of the Oedipus theme in Western culture, Moretti's *Untitled Oedipus Rex (The Infernal Machine #1 and #2)* (pp.45, 47) include images culled from such disparate sources as an ancient sculpted Sphinx and a still from Pier Paolo Pasolini's film, *Oedipus Rex*. Linder's photographic collages, *Post-mortem*, look back to the roots of this medium

fig.7

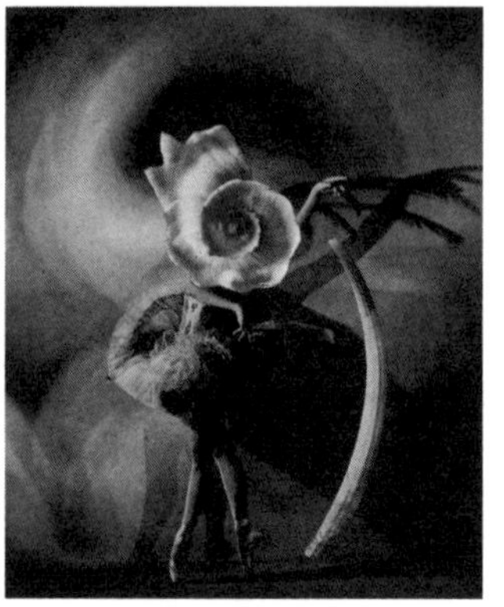

in Surrealist art. She overlays midcentury imagery of ballet dancers with natural objects – including, notably, shells and flowers, in a nod to the photographic montages of Man Ray and other Surrealist artists that enlists their potent symbolism.

The flower is a traditional metaphor of transience, the relentless turning of the life cycle. In contrast, the shell is a special reliquary that bears the form of the long disappeared being that created and inhabited it, and left its trace in its shape. We hold the shell to our ear to hear the sea within it; it contains, we imagine, a hidden, oceanic world, a metaphor for the hidden, unplumbed life of the psyche. Both home and tomb, the shell conjures an entire world.[6] *Post-mortem*, made in response to the death of Linder's mother, a dancer, evokes by its very title the determination of the cause of death via the dissection of the corpse. Its images both commemorate and discover the mourned beloved.

The ancients considered the artist's ability to conjure the dead via their painted and sculpted representations a type of magic; those that brought the dead 'back to life' earned the status of wizard. Today, representations of the dead are less fetishistic denials of death, and more insurance against forgetting it – trenchant reminders of loss. Various portraits exhibited in *The Enigma of the Hour* also recall the infrequently discussed, yet critical interlacing

6 Fittingly, tombs have often been shaped in the form of houses. See Adele Tutter, 'Melancholic relics,' in: Heide Hatry, *Icons in Ash* (Barrytown, NY: Station Hill Press, 2017), pp.134–35.

of psychoanalytic and artistic circles: for example, a core member of the Bloomsbury group Adrian Stephen, Virginia Woolf's brother, succeeded James Strachey as editor of *The International Journal of Psychoanalysis*. Displayed, too, are archival materials that richly document the controversies and compromises, the behind-the-scenes negotiations between the various individuals and factions involved in the publication of an international journal. Exhibited alongside them is a portrait of Adrian Stephen by his lover, Duncan Grant, the attribution of which, until now, was almost forgotten. (Regrettably, there is no record of the purchase of the canvas by the British Psychoanalytical Society.) Recalling Cézanne's loose brushwork and broad patches of colour, Grant conjures facets of this somber, complex man that lay concealed by a quiet interiority.

fig.8

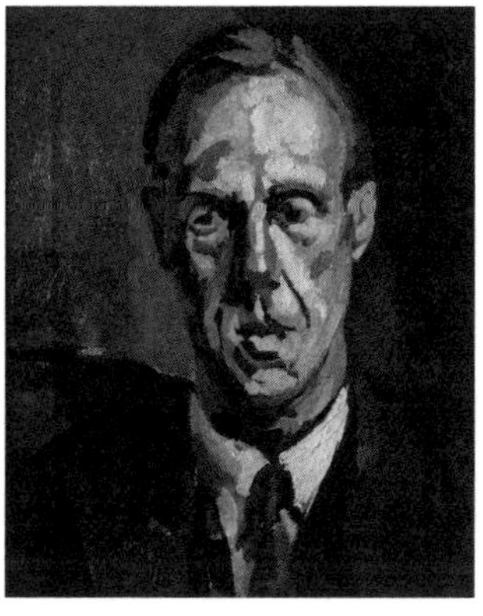

Also epitomizing the connections between psychoanalysis and the Bloomsbury group is James Strachey's role in publishing the English translation of Sigmund Freud's work. The younger brother of Lytton Strachey, he edited and translated the *Standard Edition of the Works of Sigmund Freud*, together with his wife Alix. Goshka Macuga's vase forms pays homage to the oft-unseen collaborations that underlie intellectual generativity. One, in the form of Freud's head, evokes the ancient narratives of Zeus, who gives birth to Athena through his head, and of Samson, whose power derives from his head of hair; at the same time, it plays on the archetypal image of the bearded analyst. Macuga flanks her figure of Freud with those of Alix Strachey and Joan Riviere: two women who quietly contributed to the new discipline of psychoanalysis. Riviere's coif rises in a cone of phallic power, while Strachey's face and neck are coiled with rope, suggesting that her famous reticence was not altogether voluntary.

fig.9

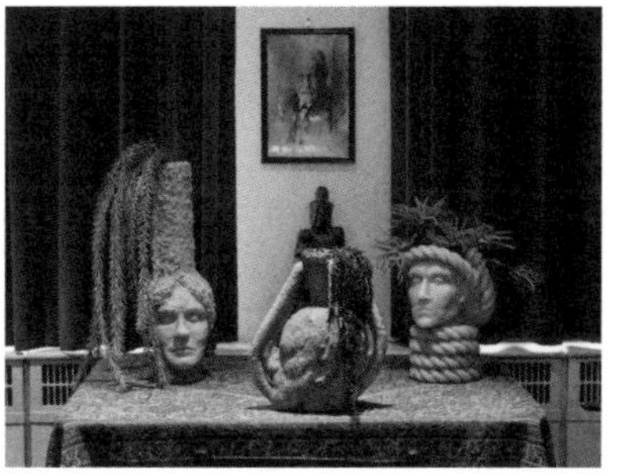

The rope in Strachey's sculpture references an early photographic portrait by Barbara Ker-Seymer and John Banting, also on display, in which Strachey's head butts up against a transparent glass cube. Invoking an umbilical cord leading to a sterile, empty vessel, Strachey appears attached to the cube by a length of thickly twisted rope, which, in Macuga's hands, becomes a choking noose. While the Ker-Seymer and Banting photograph brings attention to Strachey's role as occasional muse to the Surrealist artists in her circle, the recumbent position of its subject recalls the analysand on the analytic couch – thereby raising provocative implications for the role of the analyst, who in the past was often analogized as a 'blank screen' for the analysand's projections.

Freud advised his analysands to lie on the analytic couch to help them relax, thereby facilitating free association. It was not lost on him that the recumbent position is that in which we sleep, and in which we dream. Indeed, it could be said that the regressive, inwardly-focused and yet permeable state of mind induced by the analytic setting occupies a border zone of consciousness somewhere between waking and sleeping,[7] which, in psychoanalytic parlance, is known as 'reverie'.

7 Paradoxically, as Sarah Ackerman points out, Freud had some trepidation around theorizing this border state. See her 'Exploring Freud's Resistance to the Oceanic Feeling,' *Journal of the American Psychoanalytic Association*, 65: 9-31 (2017).

fig. 10

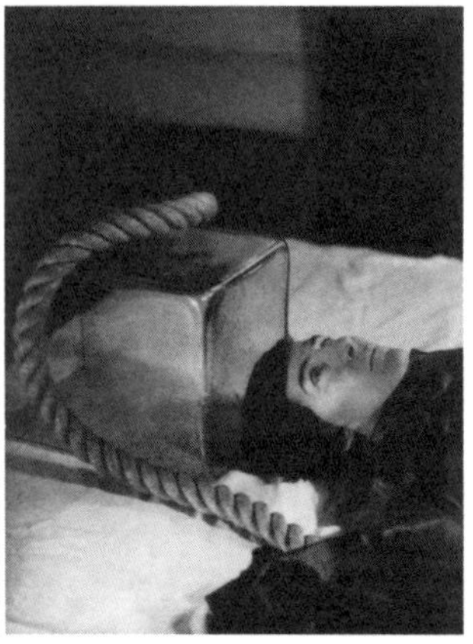

The installation of Goshka Macuga's *Somnambulist*, a realistic life-size figure of a sleeping pantomime in white-face, on a Persian rug next to Anna Freud's analytic couch, underlines its connection to the psychoanalytic setting: the sleepwalker also occupies an indeterminate state between sleep and waking. Somnambulism was a theme of increasing fascination in the late nineteenth century, in parallel to social-cultural preoccupations with hypnosis.[8] To wit, George du Maurier's 1895 novel *Trilby*, whose eponymous protagonist – a celebrated singer who could only perform when under hypnosis by the exploitative Svengali – was at the time the best selling novel in the world. Further, hypnosis and somnambulism were at the time both firmly linked to the mystery of creativity. Like the analysand and the sleepwalker, the artist draws on the unconscious mind; like the mime, the artist relies on gestural, rather than linguistic expressions. Like dreams, the

fig. 11

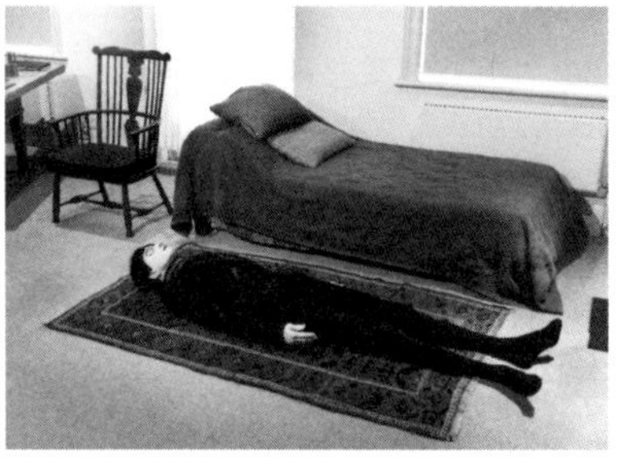

8 See Tony James, 'Somnambulism, Natural and Magnetic,' in *Dream, Creativity, and Madness in Nine-teenth Century France* (Oxford University Press, 1995), pp. 14–26.

artist's gestures, when translated into artistic productions, contain and convey meanings about which the artist may remain (at least temporarily) unaware or unconscious.

The Sphinx mingles the might of the lion with the intellect of man. In the classical myths of metamorphosis, man is transformed into all manner of shapes and things: a metaphorical embodiment of the myriad and very real transformations of life, as well as its unseen, unknown potentialities:

... imagination bodies forth
The forms of things unknown.

Paloma Varga Weisz's *Lazlo's dream*, a figure carved from limewood, is a mostly human form, but has the ears and multiple teats of a dog or other small mammal. The title of the piece suggests that this startling chimera may have been summoned by a dream, another testimony to the sustained presence of metamorphic themes in our cultural unconscious.

fig. 12

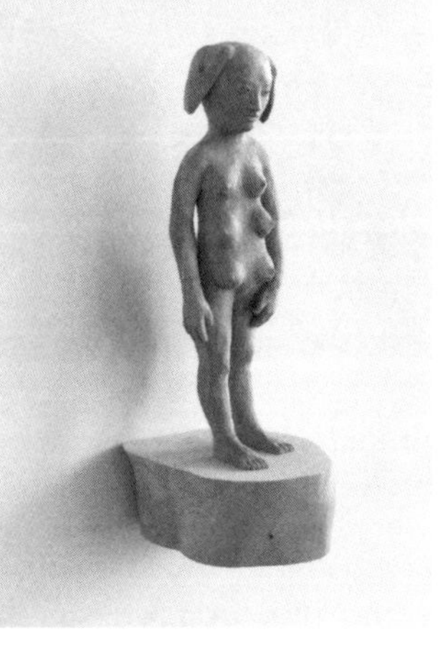

'All my works in the show are a sort of mirror to myself as well as self-portraits of a kind,' reflects Moretti. The same could be said for all art, for hard as one might try to elude the self-expression inherent in art, it is inescapable. Indeed, the form represented most often in art – the body – literally embodies the psyche; accordingly, the most frequent metonymic variation of figurative representation is the bust, which includes and focuses on the head. One of Daniel Silver's takes on classical portrait busts, *After Bath Mannequins 2*, enlists different materials to distinguish head from shoulders and chest, commenting on the seamed, yet seamless relationship between body and mind. Like Ozymandias in the desert, the pitted, eroded surface of its face reminds us that not even aesthetic representation is immortal; like the indecipherable inscriptions on old tombstones, distinguishing features eventually degrade. The exploration of our individuality reveals its inevitable limits.

fig.13

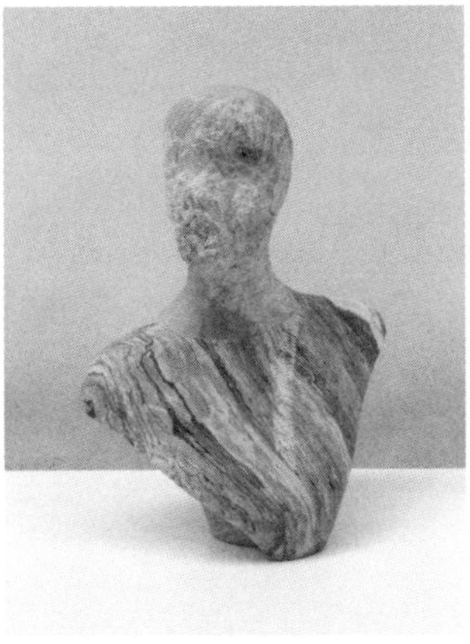

My work is about making new connections between objects and images and in my curating this is not only limited by images in a collage for example but expands further out into space establishing a conversation with the works of others or even non art – objects or settings, in this case the archive material and the atmospheric setting of Freud's house ...
– Simon Moretti

Evoking additional meaning in the associative spaces between the works of different artists, the group exhibition mirrors facets of our culture, offering a glimpse of the state of our shared psyche, the mind of our place and time.

If art and psychoanalysis afford us access to the inner world, the cultural matrix in which art incubates is an expression of the collective unconscious. If man's artistic products survive us, culture is even longer-lived: culture *is* the collective unconscious, an immortal, yet constantly shifting living being, ever evolving and transforming.

fig.14

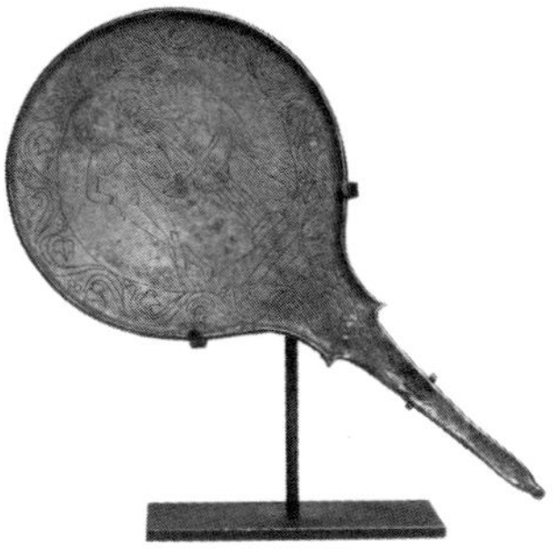

fig.1 Jean Auguste Dominique Ingres, *Oedipus and The Sphinx*, 1808.
fig.2 Marion Millner, *A Thought Too Big for Its Concept*, 1990.
fig.3 Edmund Engelman, Photograph of Berggasse 19 interior, Vienna, 1938.
fig.4 Female Sphinx amulet, seated with hair in cruciform design, Egyptian, Late Period 712-323BC, Museum no. 3839. Collection of the Freud Museum London.
fig.5 Medal gifted to Sigmund Freud on his 50th birthday 1906, with Freud on one side and Oedipus and the Sphinx on the other, designed by Carl Maria Schwerdtner.
g.6 Simon Moretti, *Only Day and Night*, 2019.
fig.7 Linder, *Post-mortem, Alexandra (i)*, 2016.
fig.8 Duncan Grant, *Adrian Stephen*, c.late 1930s–mid 1940s.
fig.9 Goshka Macuga, *International Institute of Intellectual Co-operation, Riviere*, 2019, *International Institute of Intellectual Co-operation, Freud*, 2016, *International Institute of Intellectual, Co-operation, Strachey*, 2019.
fig.10 Barbara Ker-Seymer and John Banting, *Alix Strachey*, 1930.
fig.11 Goshka Macuga, *Somnambulist*, 2006.
fig.12 Paloma Varga Weisz, *Lazlo's dream*, 2018.
fig.13 Daniel Silver, *After Bath Mannequins* 2, 2018.
fig.14 Mirror, Bronze, Etruscan, 350–250 BC. Museum no. 3324. Collection of the Freud Museum London.

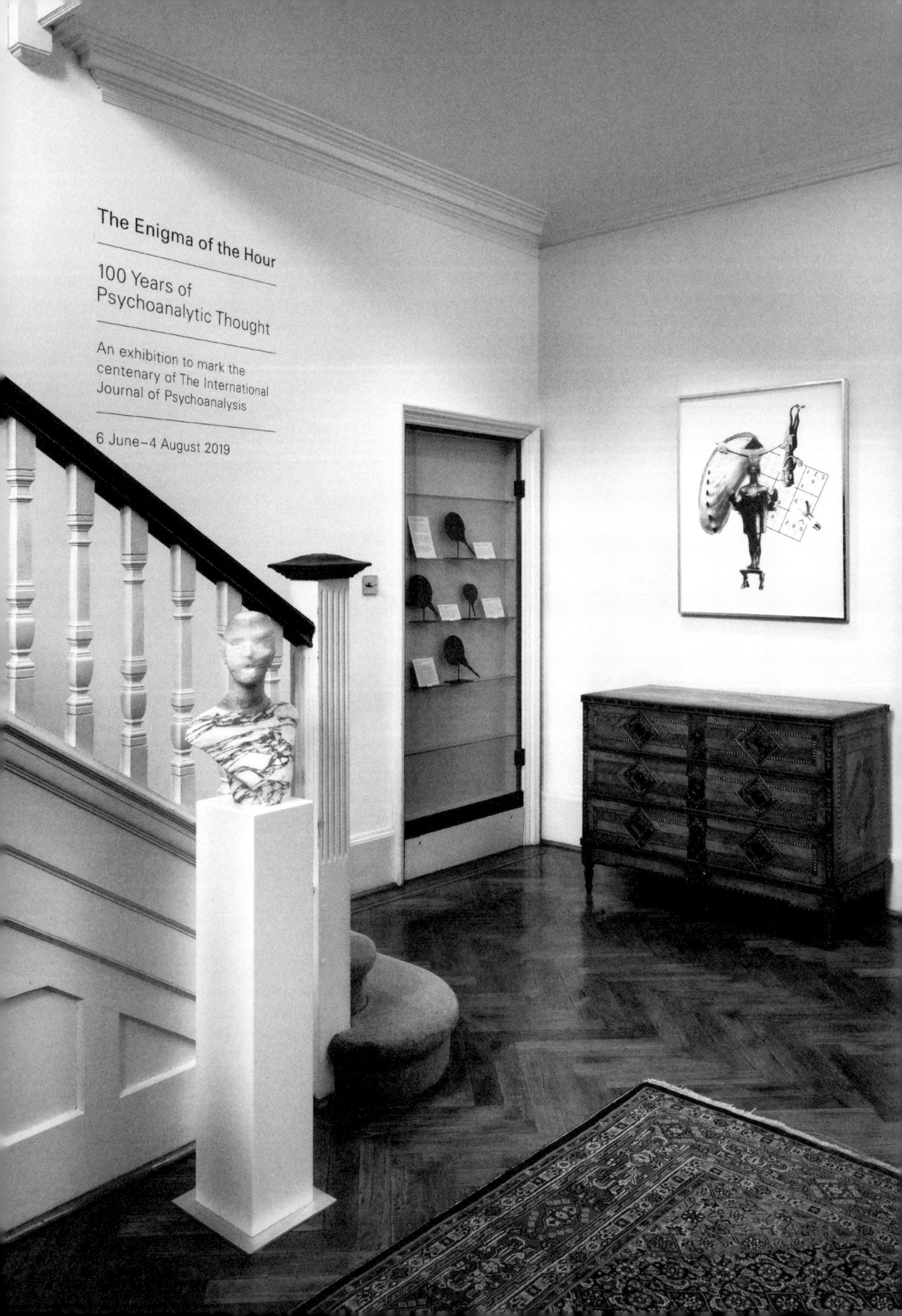

The Enigma of the Hour
100 Years of Psychoanalytic Thought
An exhibition to mark the centenary of The International Journal of Psychoanalysis
6 June–4 August 2019

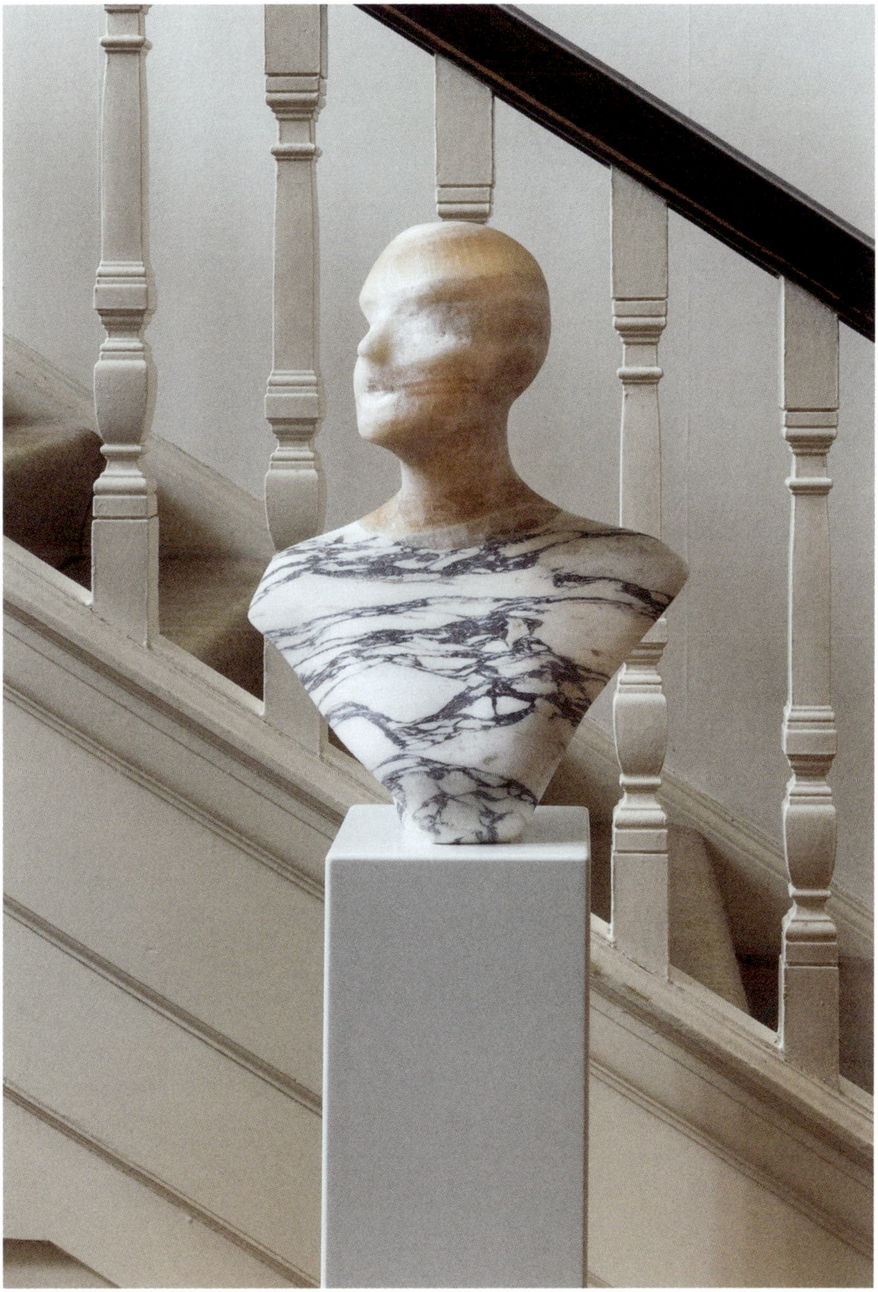

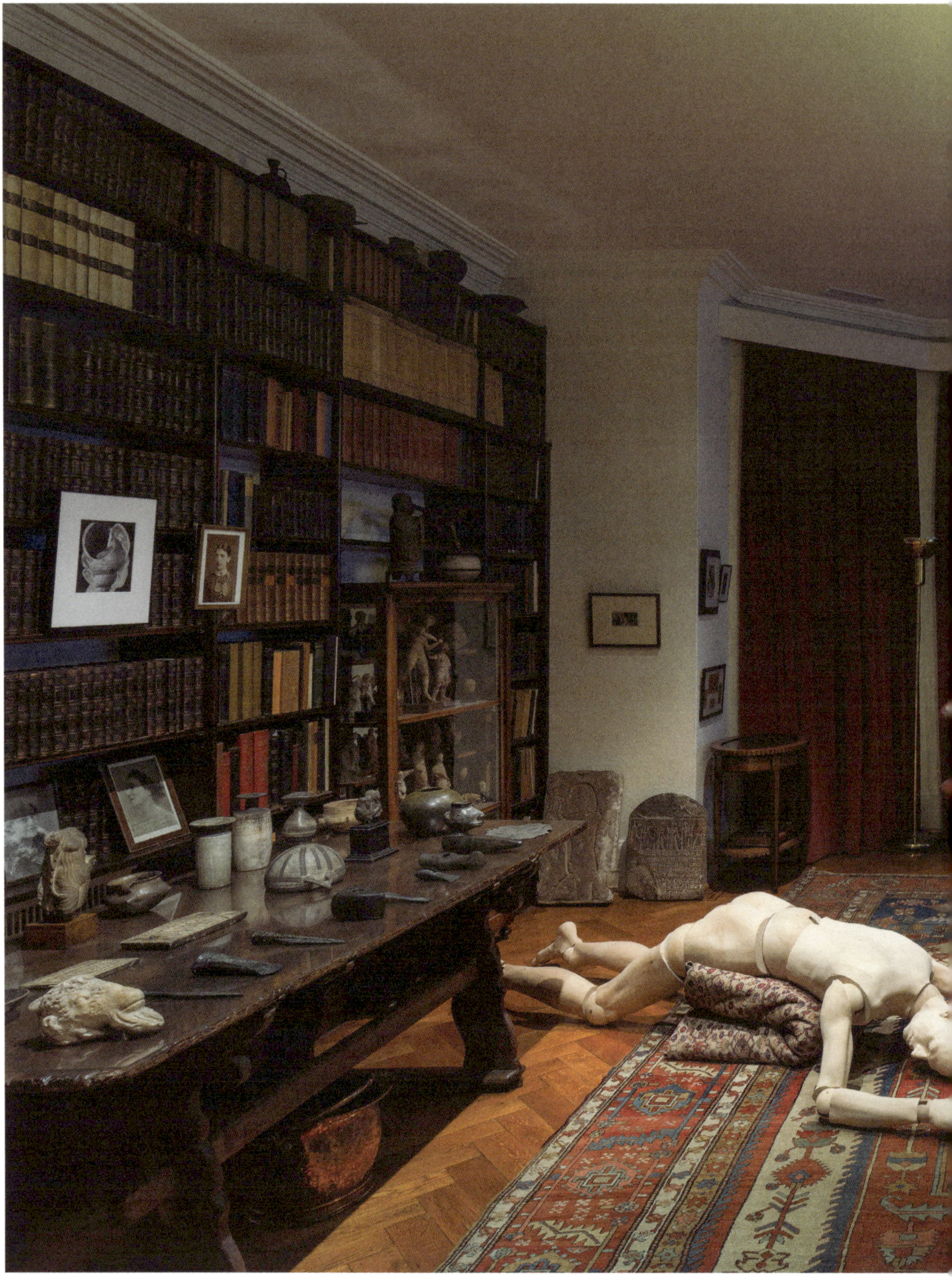

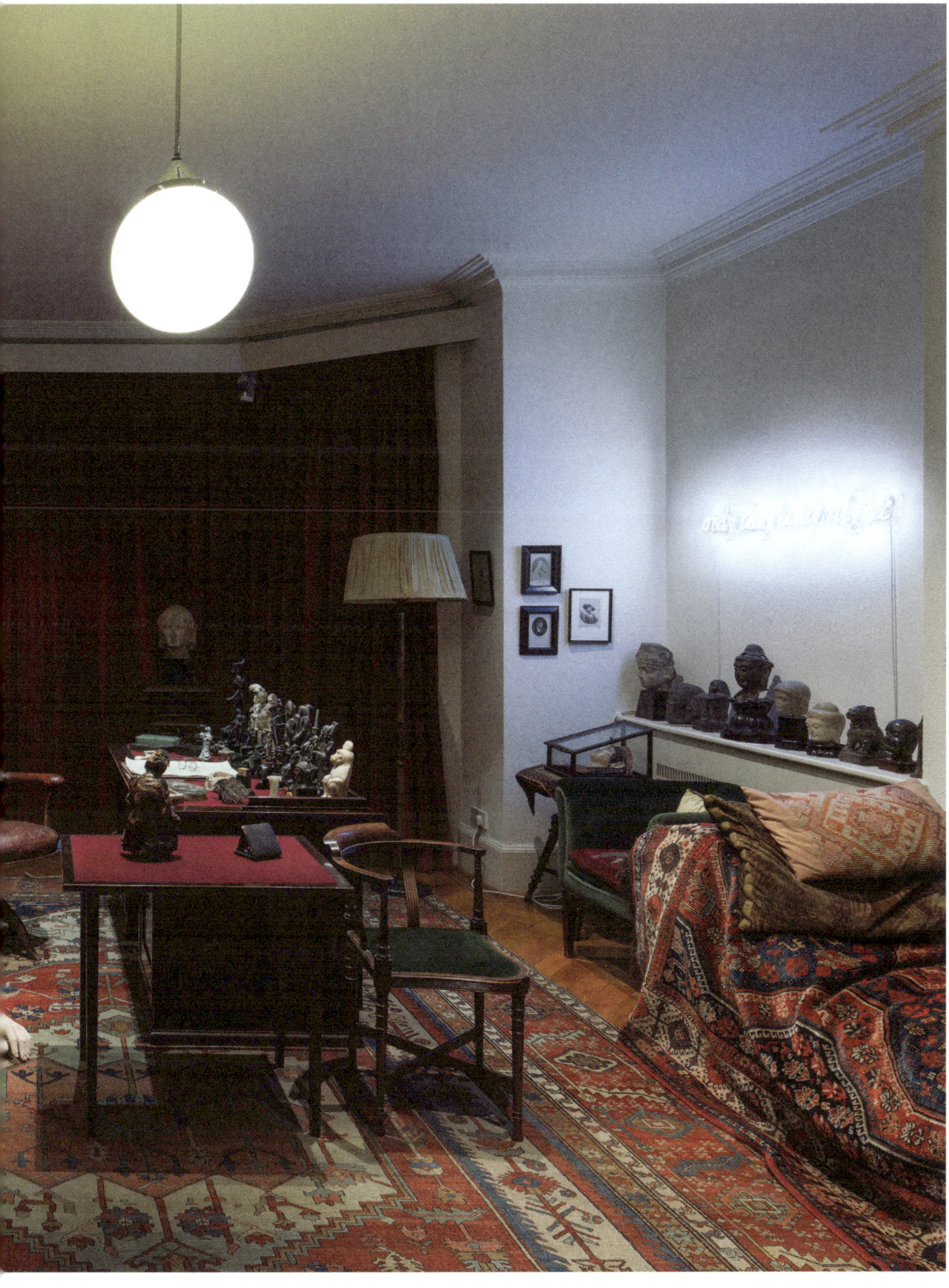

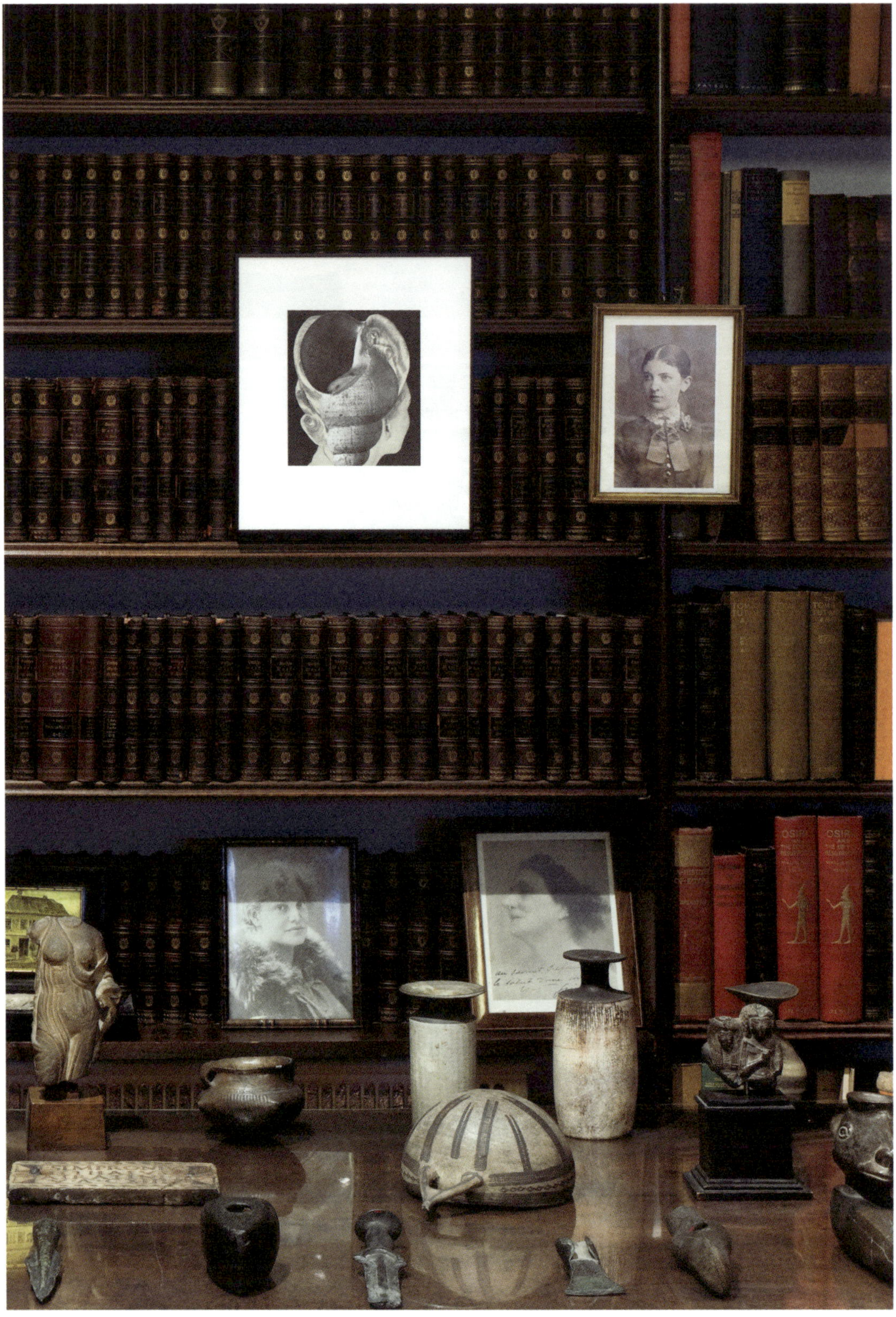

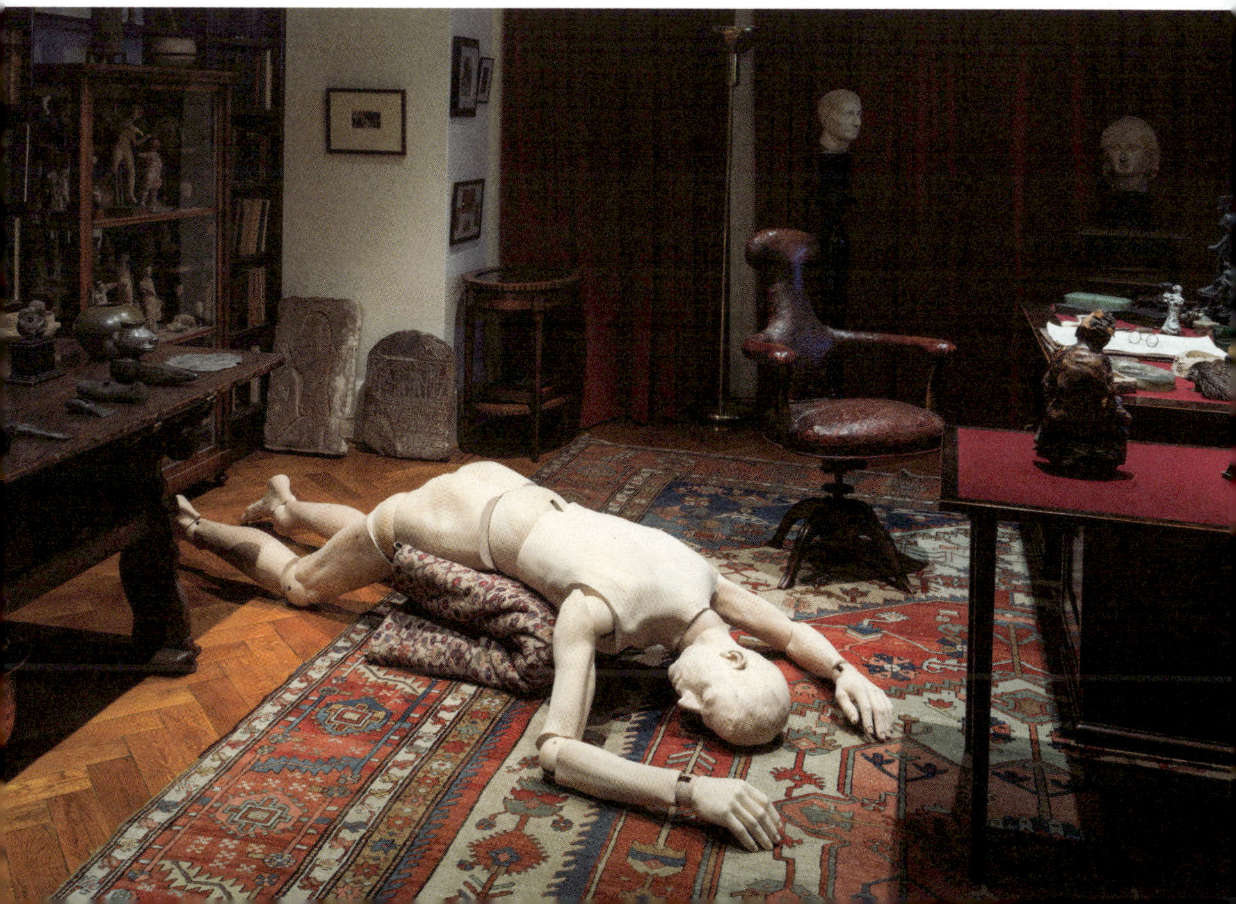

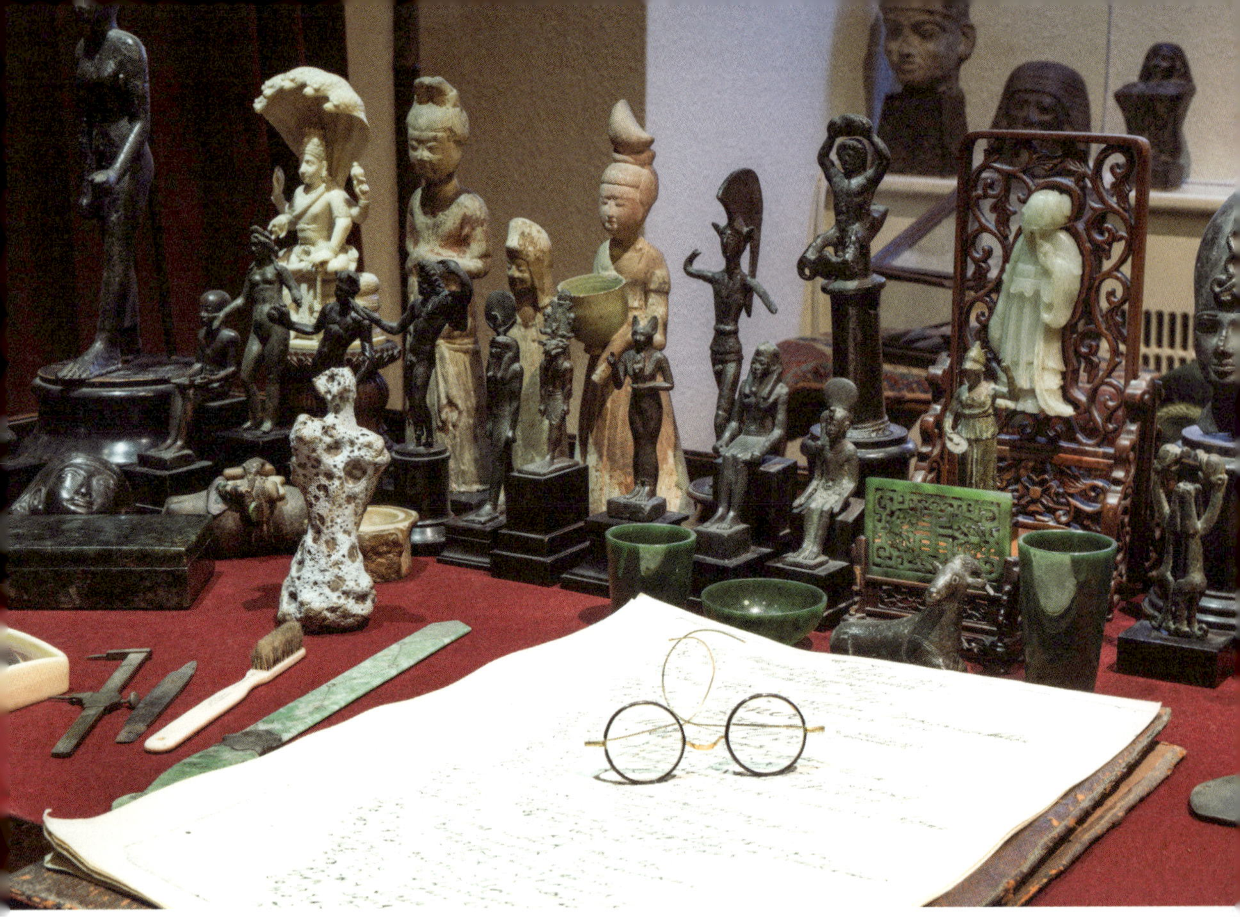

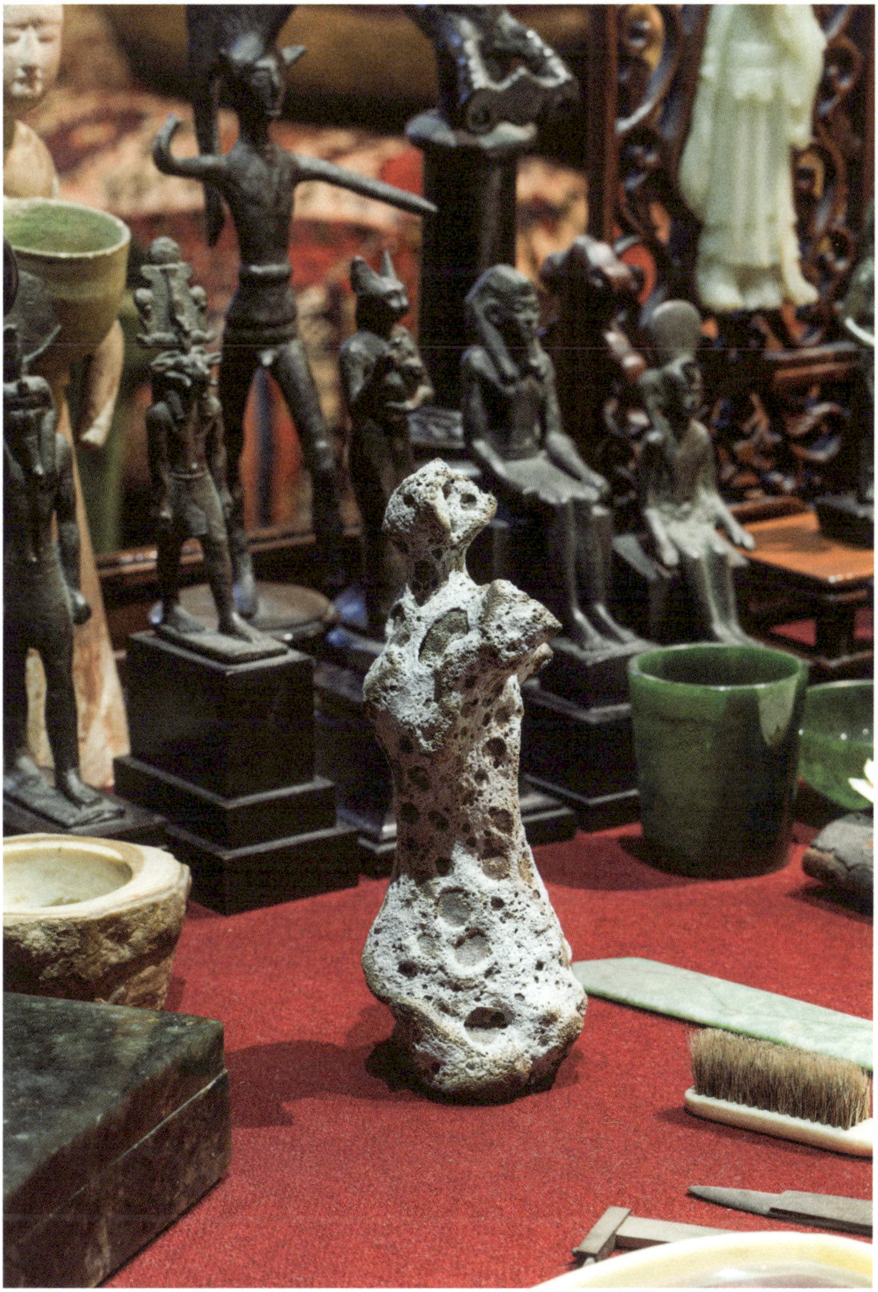

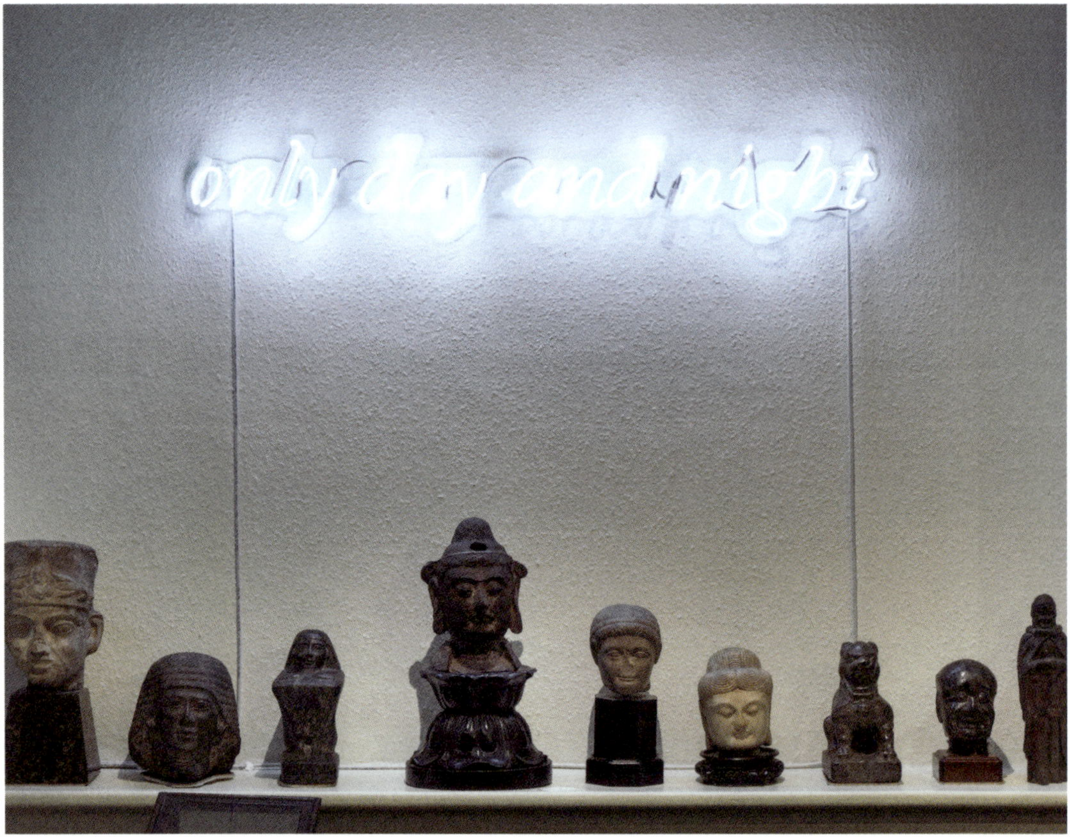
only day and night

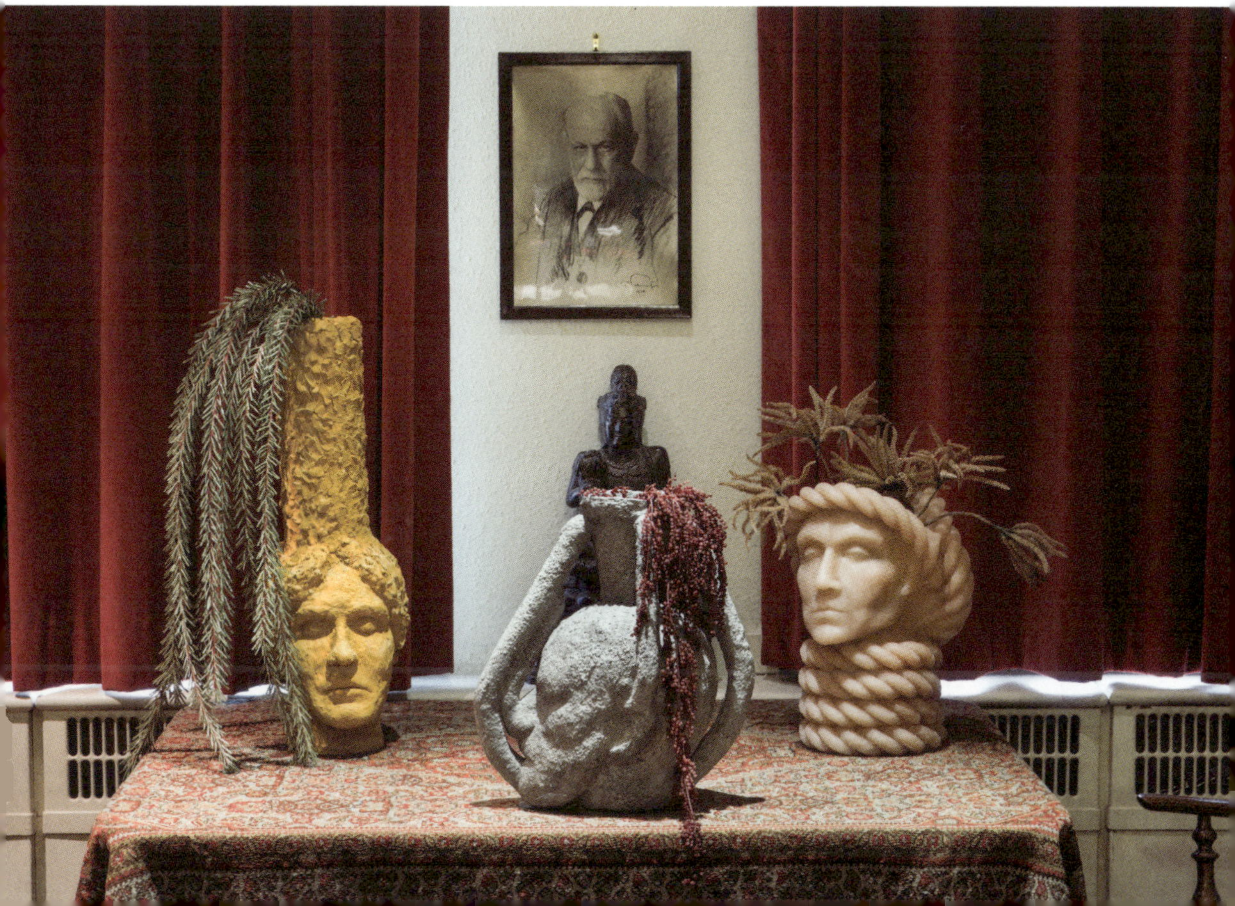

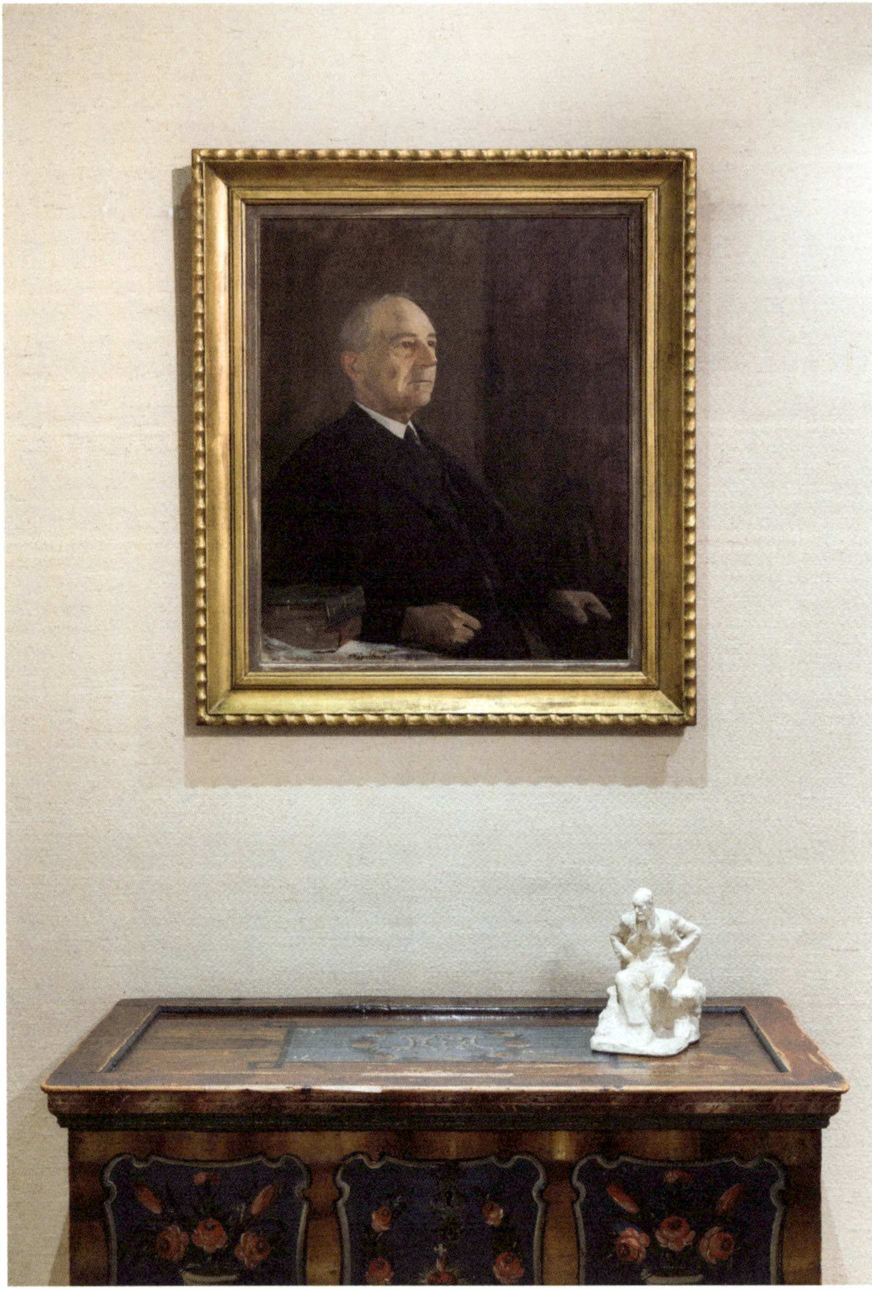

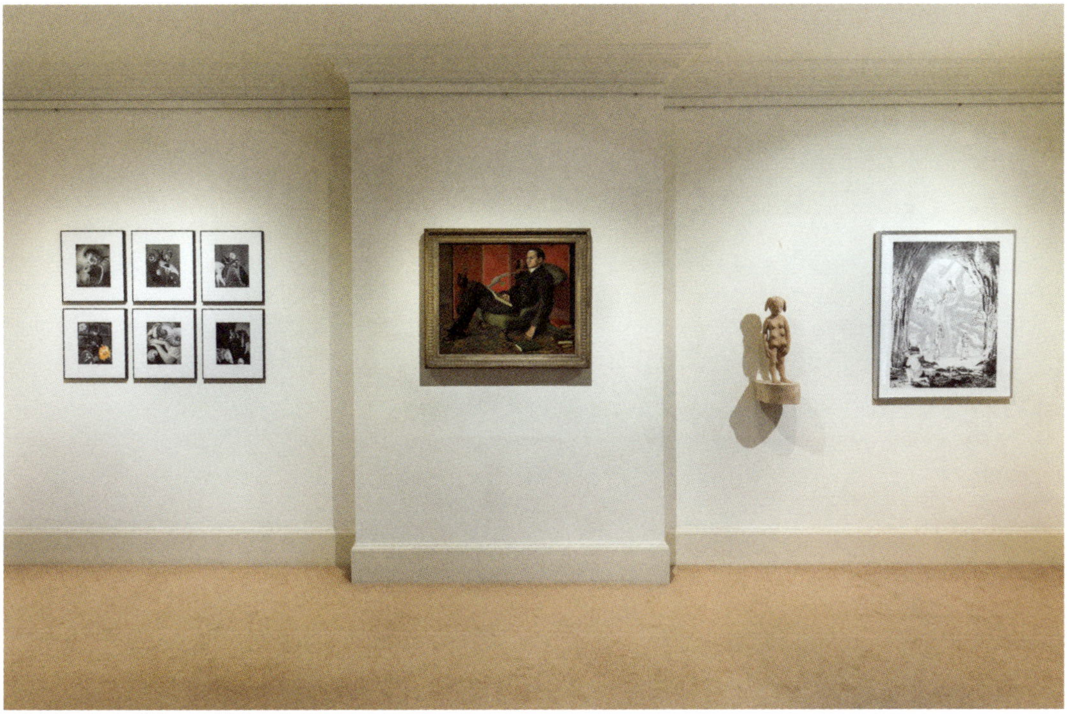

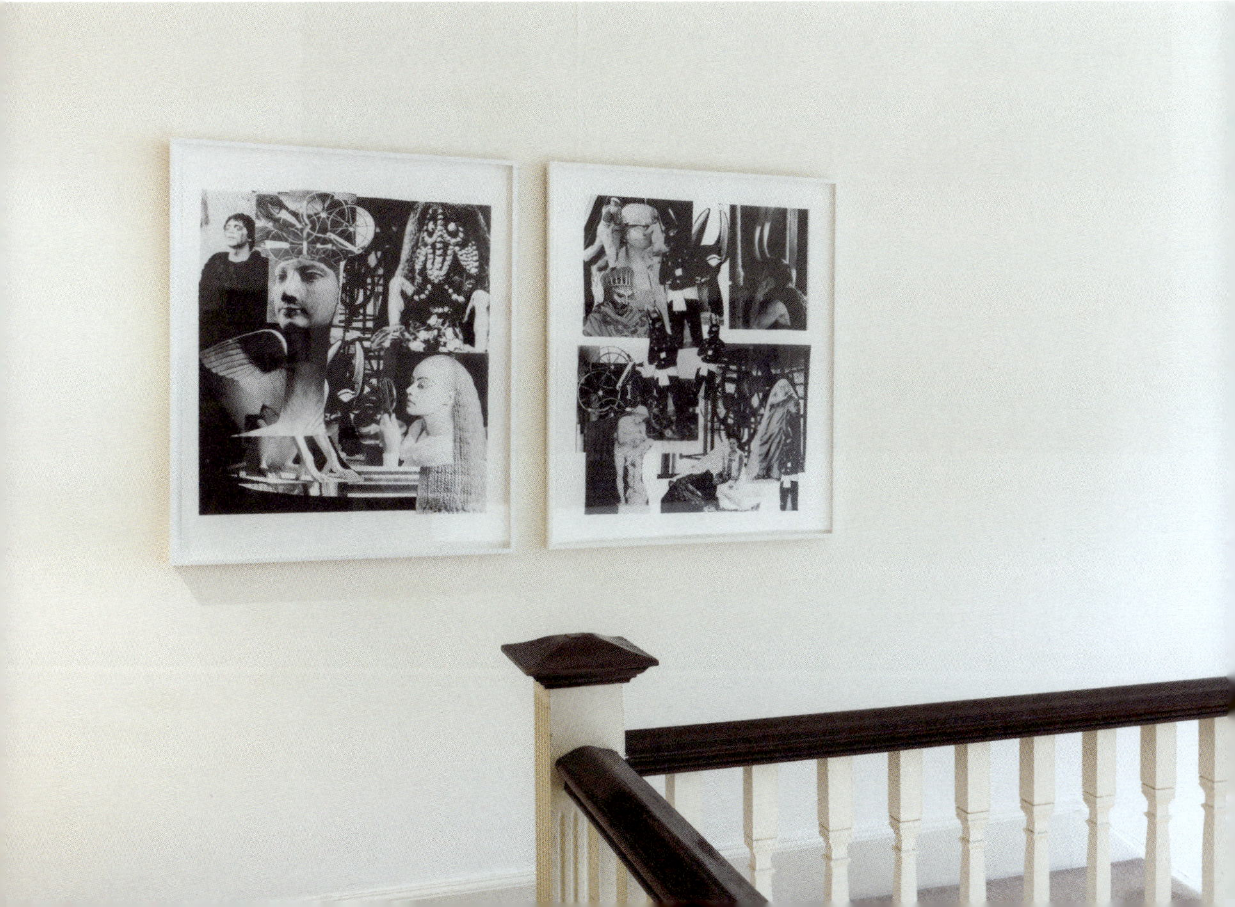

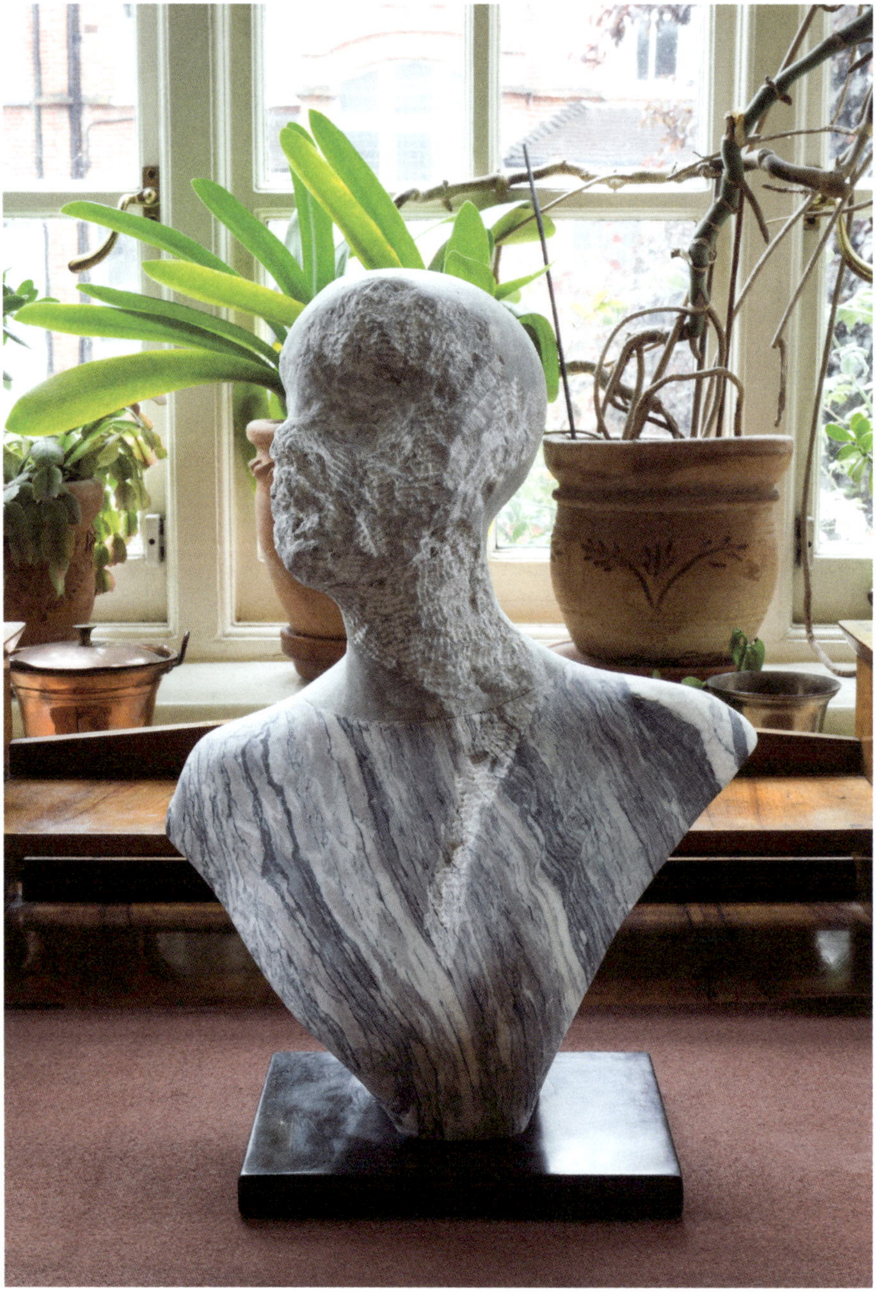

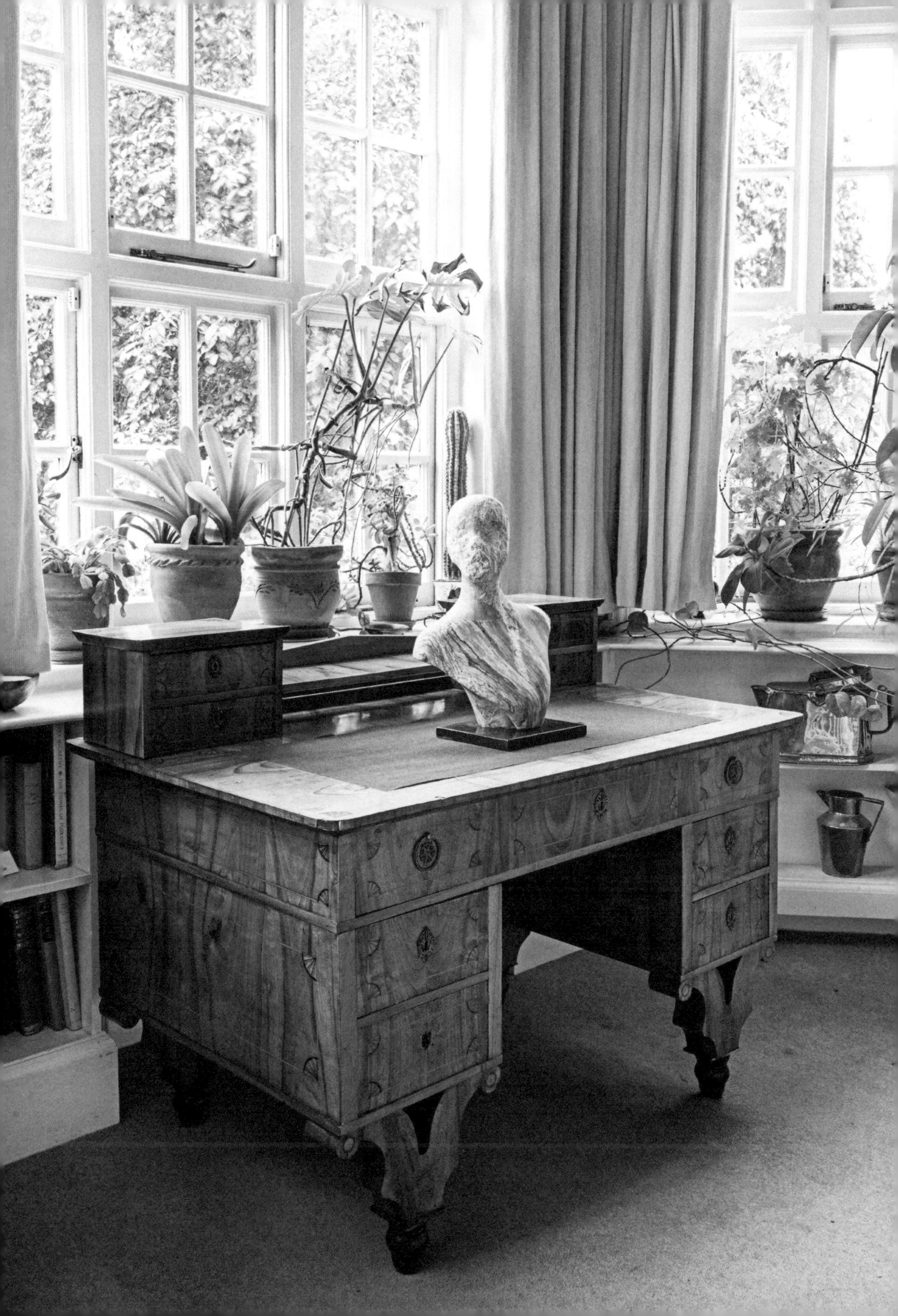

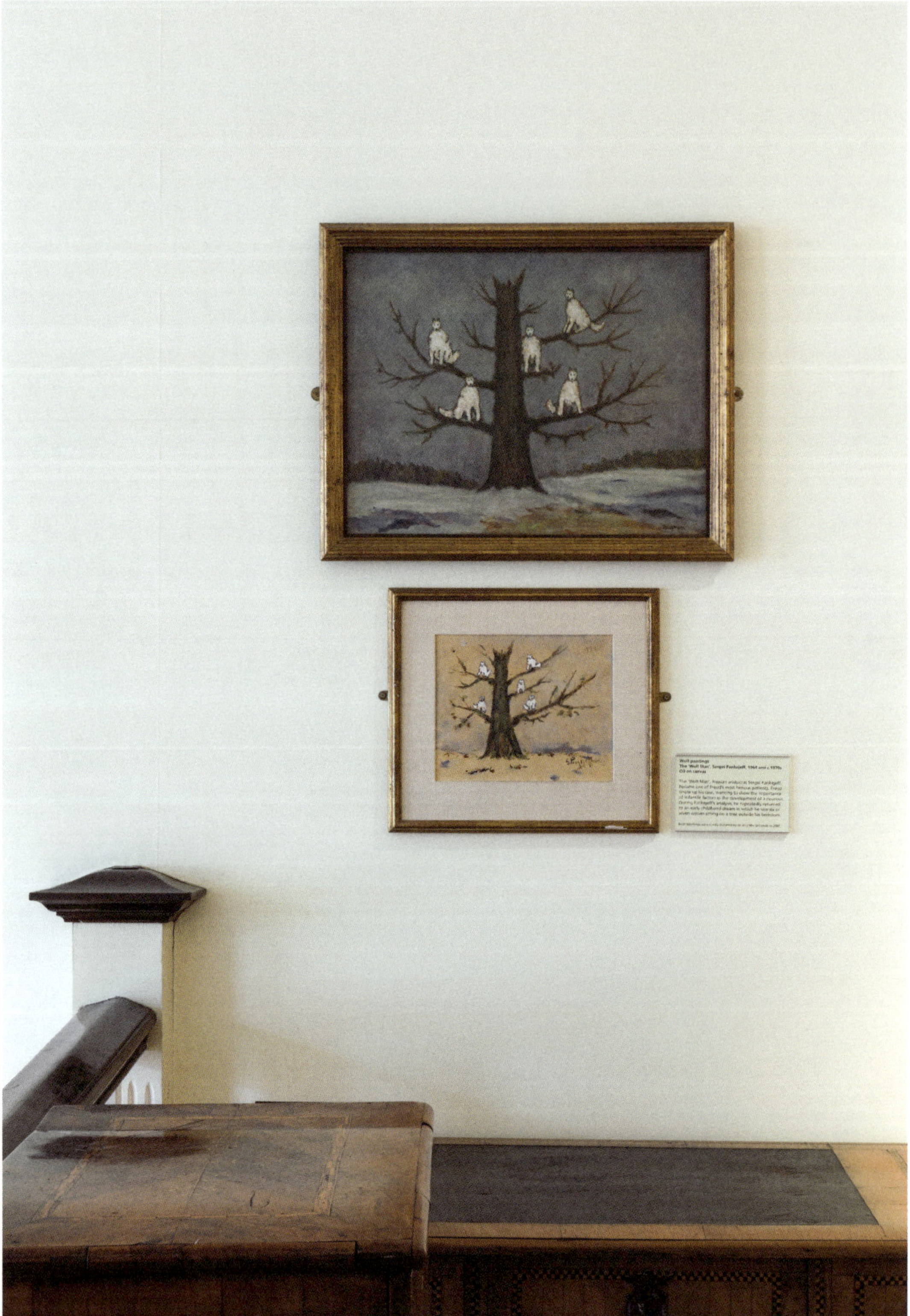
Wolf paintings
Oil on canvas

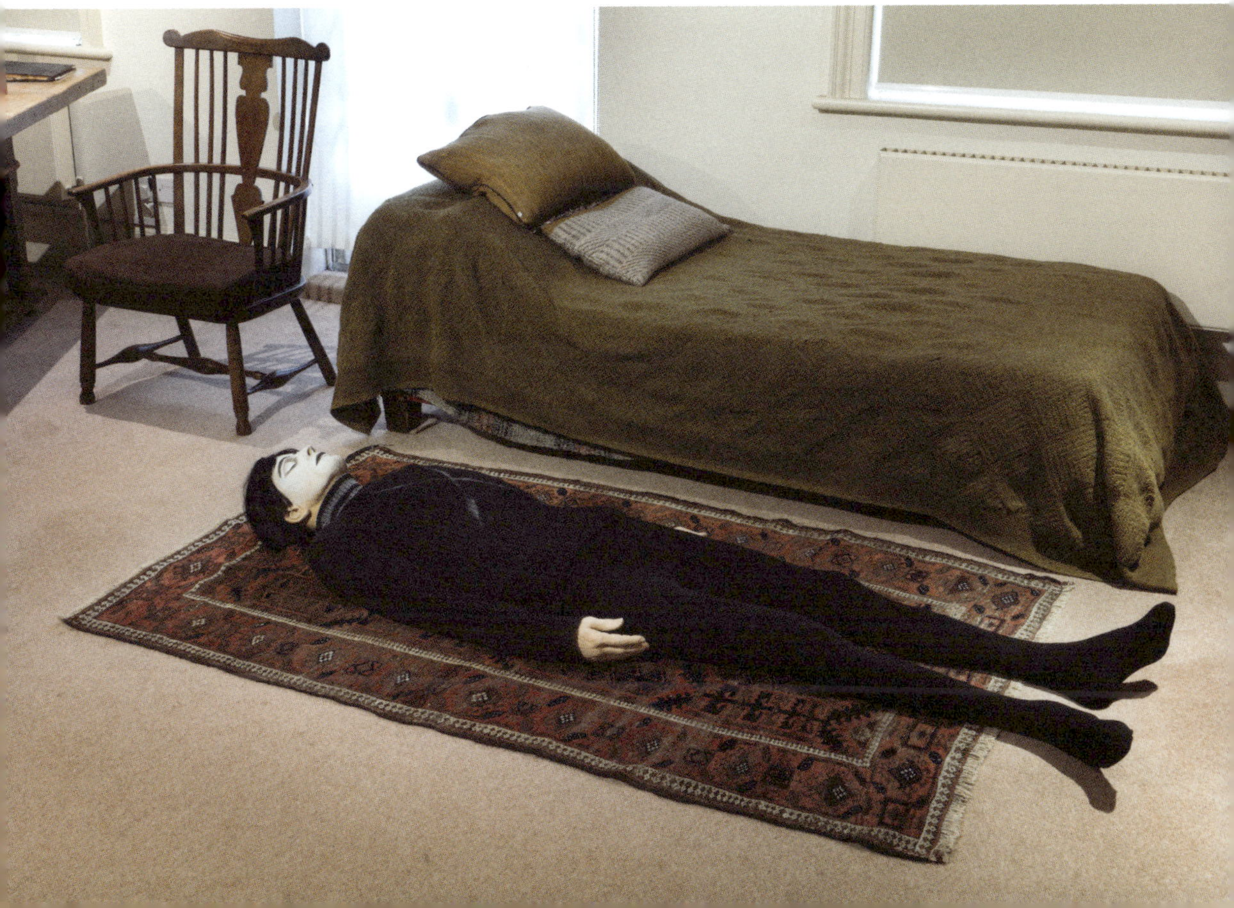

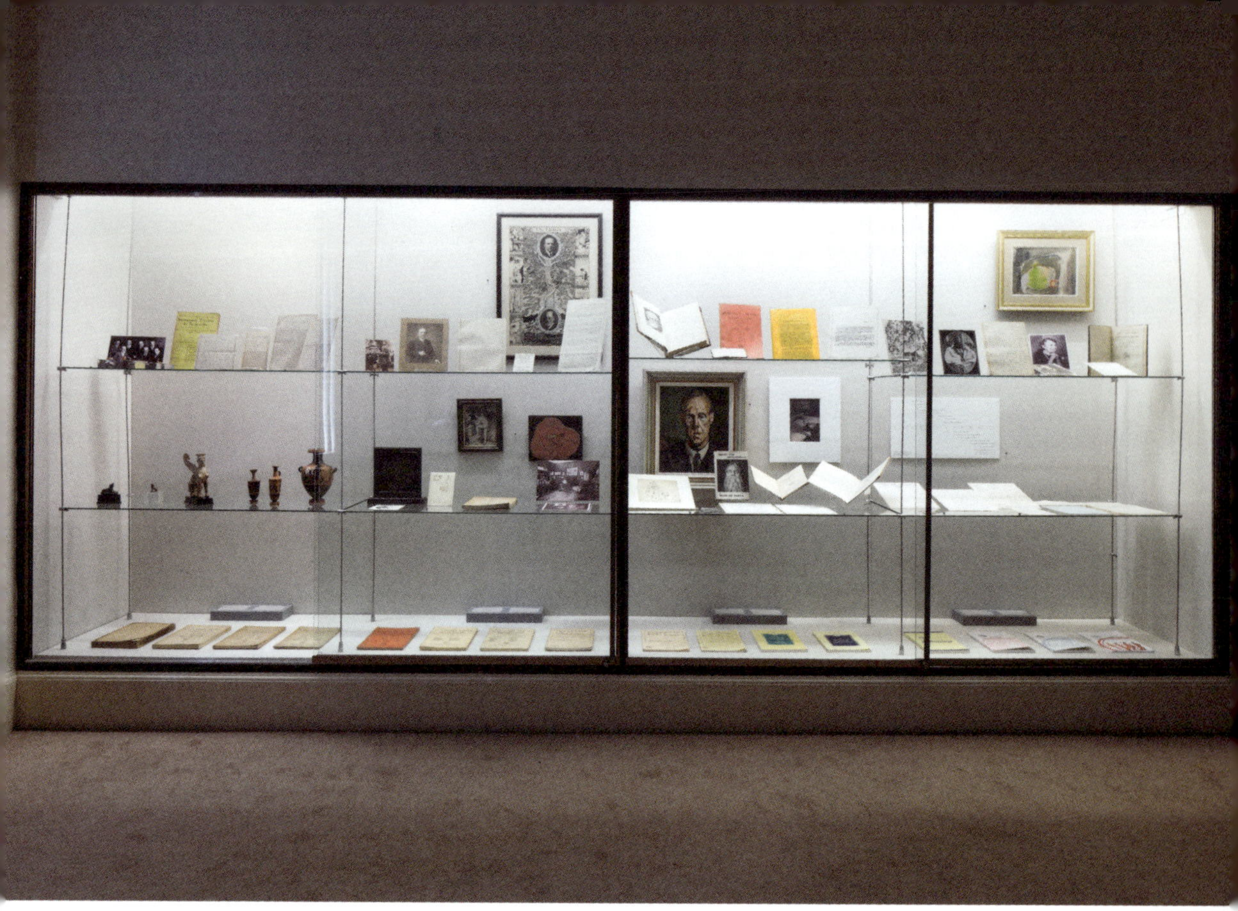

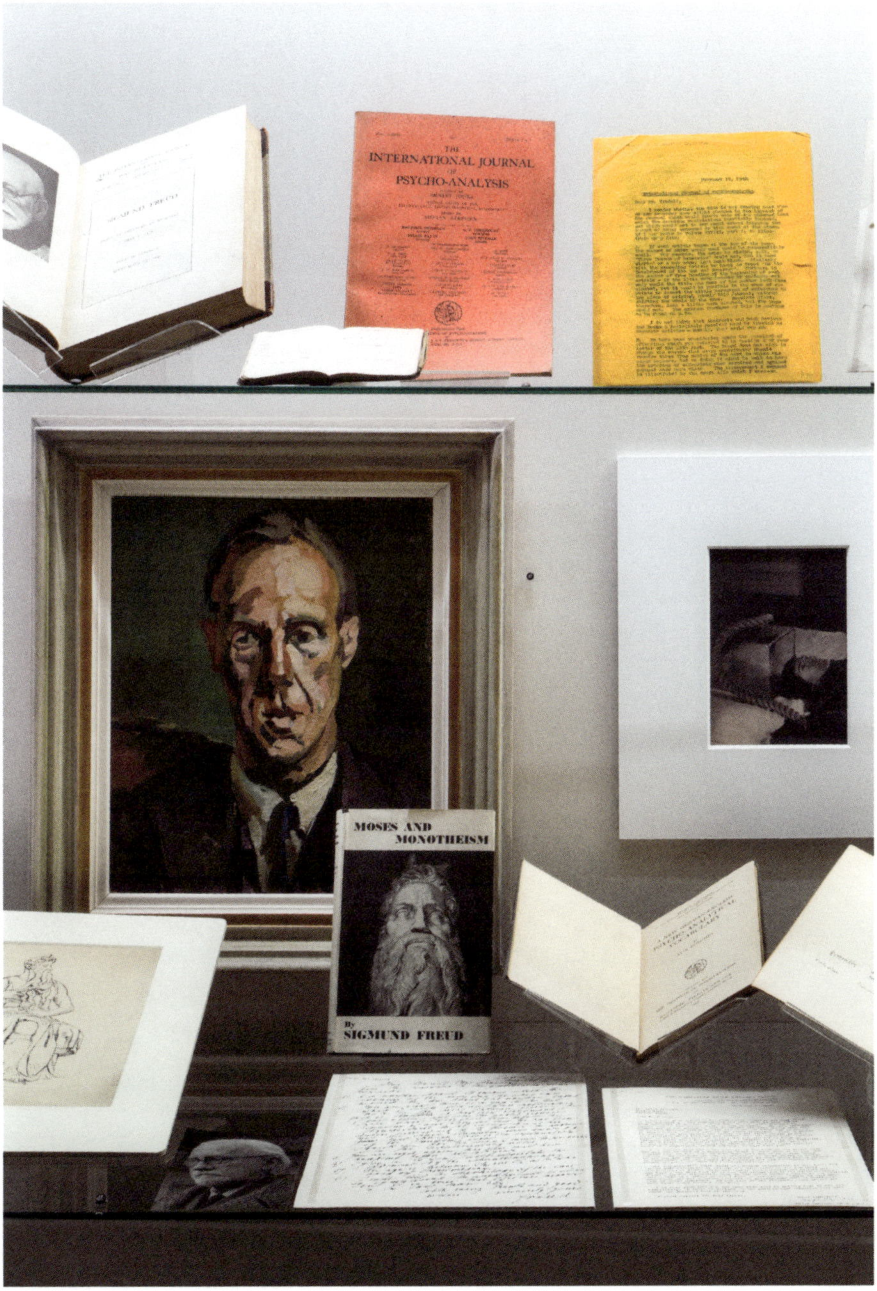
THE
INTERNATIONAL JOURNAL
OF
PSYCHO-ANALYSIS
MOSES AND
MONOTHEISM
By
SIGMUND FREUD

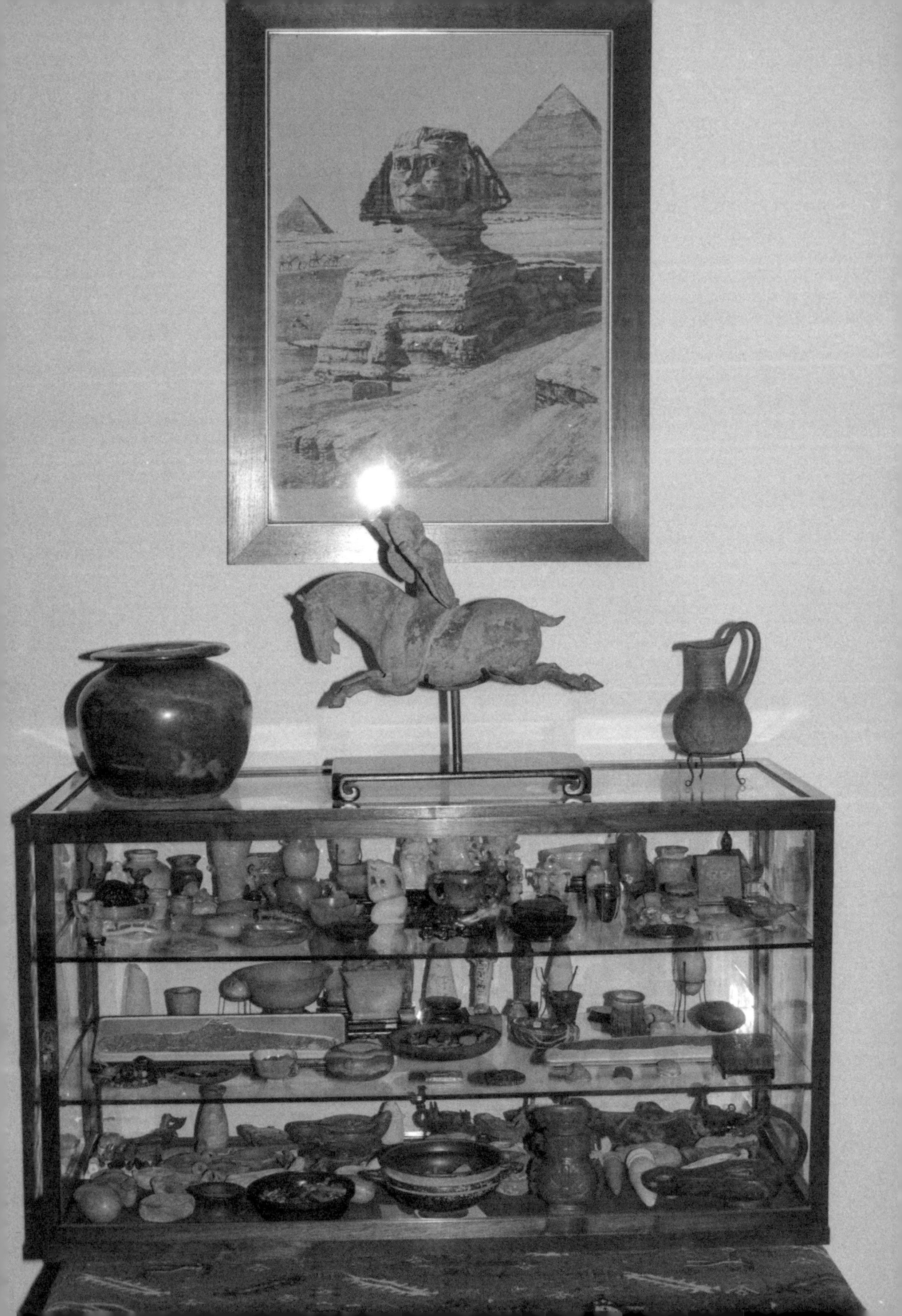

Towards the close of Flaubert's novel, *The Temptation of St Antony* (1874), the visionary hermit, assailed by demons, is pondering the nature of reality and illusion. His hallucinations are products of fantasy, 'primordial figures, whose bodies are only images.' He yearns to see them, because they can lead him to understand, he thinks, 'the link between matter and thought that constitutes Being!' (Des figures primordiales, dont les corps ne sont que les images. Si on pouvait les voir on connaitrait le lien de la matière et de la pensée, en quoi l'Etre consiste!)

As he meditates on these mysteries, the Sphinx, his neighbour in the Thebaid, appears to him, comes into view, stretched out in the sand across the Nile, drawing indecipherable letters in the sand and muttering 'I'm keeping my secret. I am dreaming and calculating.' (Je garde mon secret. Je songe et je calcule.) Above this fantastic creature, the saint sees another mythological monster from the Greek repertory: leaping and snorting fire, lashing her dragon's tail against her wings, and twisting around in the air barking loudly: the Chimaera! Her very name has come to mean illusion. By contrast to the recumbent, pensive sphinx, the Chimaera is light and joyful (légère et joyeuse) and she proclaims, 'I reveal to men dazzling perspectives with paradises in the clouds and far distant happiness. I pour into their souls unending madness, projects of bliss, plans for the future, dreams of glory, and the vows of love and virtuous resolutions... If I notice somewhere a man whose spirit rests in wisdom, I pounce on him, and strangle him.'[1]

This verbal jousting between the Sphinx and the Chimaera has become a celebrated scene from Flaubert's novel.[2] It's a duel between wisdom and folly, yet both monsters are enigmas, creatures of mystery, the projections of human fantasy, and spurs to endless delusion – which in one case leads to profound despondency, and in the other to giddy pleasure. The Sphinx is overcome by the Chimaera's seductions and begs to be released from sadness: this philosophical animal desires syzygy with frivolity and charm. However, even as the volatile chimaera promises the earth, and instructs the Sphinx to mount on her back and fly away with her, the Sphinx cannot move, but sinks deeper into the sand under the weight of melancholy and disappears.

For Flaubert the Chimaera is fantasy, her frenzied antics the movement of desire, energy, craziness, lightness and desire; she is treacherous deception but also vital, the life force that can deflect depression. Flaubert gives her the better part: she can lift human beings out of hopelessness, whereas weightier questions, as pursued by the Sphinx, are fated to be frustrated and lead to self-destruction. In French *chimère* is a feminine noun, and his Chimaera has all the charms, wiliness and treachery conventionally attributed to the female sex (la donna è mobile). Unexpectedly, the French say *le sphinx* and to some extent Flaubert's monster is a self-portrait: the serious artist weighed down by failure. The whole kinetic confrontation of the two monsters has a mock solemnity, touched with a feeling of absurdity; Flaubert can't help undercutting with his habitual sardonic scepticism the pathos of the holy hermit's torments. Yes, in spite of this bathos, the conflict between the Sphinx and the Chimaera reveals how reason can never extricate itself from the seductions of fantasy – as Freud, born in 1856, a generation before Flaubert's fable was published – recognised more lucidly than the French novelist; his view has prevailed and shaped subsequent understanding of creative imagination and its power.

The dialogue between the two mythological beings also dramatizes divergent ways of existing in time: the Sphinx embodies stability and endurance, lying along a continuum that leads ineluctably to extinction; the Chimaera's

1 Gustave Flaubert, *La Tentation de Saint Antoine* (Paris: Gallimard, 1967), pp.238–41.

2 Their opposition is sharpened in French, where, unlike Greek and Latin and most other languages, the sphinx is male in gender.

rhythm is quick and syncopated, her volatility takes up each moment and fills it with difference, her restless motion mimics the vagaries of human consciousness in action, 'untameable caprice'. Freud generally acknowledged his debt to fiction, and Theodor Reik, one of his first students and protegés, wrote his PhD on *The Temptation of Saint Antony*, so Flaubert's work was certainly known to him. But Freud's view of the Sphinx differs profoundly from Flaubert's. This Egyptian figure of a human-headed, lion-bodied monster plays a major part in his thought, and in the imagery he adopted for his science. He chose the scene of Oedipus' encounter with the Sphinx for the image fig.15 on the seal of the *Journal of Psycho-analytical Studies*; for Freud, the Sphinx's fatal poser went to the heart of the matter ('the riddle where babies come from (This, in a distorted form...,' writes Freud in Infantile Sexuality, 'is the same riddle that was propounded by the Theban Sphinx.)'[3] When Simon Moretti began thinking about ways of celebrating the journal's centenary, he took his cue from this image, which is derived from a monumental painting by Ingres, but as the exhibition reveals, Freud collected Sphinxes.

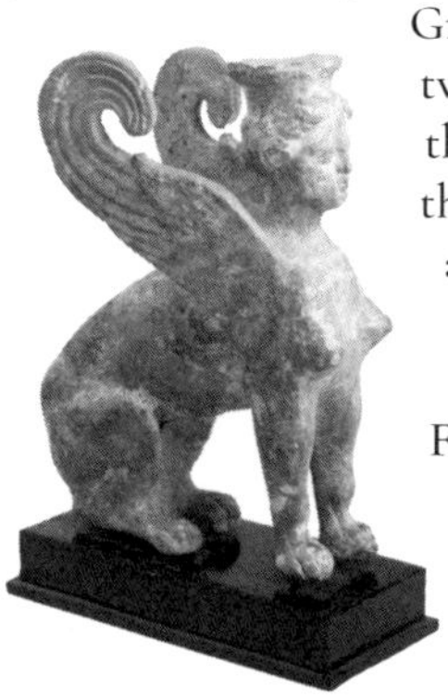

In response to Freud's last house and his collections of antiquities, Moretti has plied together several strands of thought. The exhibition juxtaposes classical and near Eastern antiquities – antique statuettes of divinities, precious gems with amuletic images of creatures – from the array Freud assembled close by him in his consulting room; these then resonate with archival materials from the journal, and portraits and photographs of his associates. The title of the show and of this accompanying book comes from a painting by Giorgio de Chirico, who is a recurring figure of inspiration in Moretti's work. *The Enigma of the Hour* alludes to profound questions about being in relation to time, but also, more particularly, invokes the temporality and the quest for meaning within the conventional psychoanalytic 'hour'. Co-curated by Moretti with the artist Goshka Macuga and the Journal's editor-in-chief, Dana Birksted-Green, the show at the Freud Museum London in many ways enacts the psychoanalytic method, offering symbolic scenes and objects in associative conjunctions to detonate intense moments of recognition, as patterns emerge and buried meanings rise.

Members of Freud's inner circle are represented in various media, from traditional oils painted from life (*James Strachey* by Duncan Grant, 1910, p.53), to Macuga's vivid twists on certain Greek vases (p.21), those Kantharoi and Oinochoea in the shape of portrait busts; her heads as drinking horns relate to a project called the *International Institute of Intellectual Cooperation* (2016). Sigmund Freud, Alix Strachey and Joan Riviere are included in this pantheon. The show also acknowledges several more women besides the celebrated figure of Anna Freud. Marjorie Brierley and Marion Milner were actively involved with the Journal, and with the psychoanalytical movement in Britain in the formative years. Milner is represented by a significant painting entitled *A Thought Too Big for Its Concept* (1990, p.80), which posits, I think, that an artist's vision (or 'thought') can step beyond the boundary of rational tenets ('concept'). Milner wrote illuminatingly – and presciently – about the therapeutic potential of artistic expression in her book, *On Not Being Able to Paint* (1950) and *In the Hands of the Living God* (1969), in which she dwells on the case of a patient, Susan.[4]

In previous curatorial interventions, such as *Revolt of the Sage* (2017), Simon Moretti gathered around him many elective affines, living and dead, each participant adding a facet to the work of the whole, like a living

3 Sigmund Freud, 'Infantile Sexuality', in: Sigmund Freud and Angela Richards (ed.), *On Sexuality. Three Essays on the Theory of Sexuality and Other Works*, trans. James Strachey (Harmondsworth: Penguin, 1977), pp.88–126.

4 Mary Jacobus, *The Poetics of Psychoanalysis in the Wake of Klein* (Oxford: Oxford University Press, 2005), pp.119–29.

collage, which amounts to a pleasurable enigma in itself.[5] Exposition as in a scientific experiment is not the primary motive for the artist-curator, but rather a poetic assemblage of elements which spark further connections and associations in relation to one another, in the same way that a colour, set against a different colour will change subtly, and then gain another character by contrast with yet another colour, and so forth (as in Josef Albers' exercises in complementaries).

Like the Sphinx and the Chimaera, artists are on the whole inhabitants of endless puzzlement. Enigma isn't a comfortable place, but it is an aesthetic vocation.

II Tangled Time

The Sphinx's riddle seems too elementary to have defeated so many: 'What walks on four legs in the morning, two legs at midday and three legs in the evening?' Oedipus has no difficulty, and answers: 'A Man'. In other versions, her question ends 'and speaks with a single voice?' This is an interesting, overlooked addition, for it draws attention to a person's unified consciousness over a lifetime, one of the central tenets of the Judaeo-Christian – and Freudian – model of the psyche. The paradox is that a compact, brief formula like a riddle can encompass vistas of past, present and future. When Oedipus gives the correct answer, the Sphinx is so crushed that, according to some sources, she throws herself off a cliff in despair. She has come face to face with a human being who embodies a contradiction of the law that decrees that someone cannot be at the same time their own child's sibling or their own parent's spouse. Yet Oedipus who sees so clearly and replies so readily, can't see that he himself tangles up proper generational succession.

Popular riddles the world over often relish the knots and tangles of family relationships and play with the deficiencies of language in clarifying them:

Brother and sisters have I none, but this man's father is my father's son. Who am I?

Some medieval riddles, recorded in the folklore surrounding the Queen of Sheba's visit to King Solomon, when she tested his wisdom with hard questions, focus on Lot and his daughters. For example, she asks the wise king,

'A woman said to her son, thy father is my father, and thy grandfather my husband; thou art my son, and I am thy sister.' Solomon answers straightaway that the speaker is one of Lot's daughters addressing her son.[6]

Another example, from the Anglo-Saxon Exeter Book, also relishes the tangle of relations in the Bible story:

A man sat down to feast with two wives, / Drank wine with two daughters, supped with two sons. / The daughters were sisters with their own two sons, / Each son a favoured, first-born prince. / The father of each prince sat with his son, / Also the uncle and nephew of each.[7]

Both these instances reveal the deep connection between the riddle as a form, the enigma the Sphinx poses, and Oedipus's tragic outcast destiny. That incest disrupts proper order of time and society also governs the plot of *Pericles*, one of Shakespeare's late 'romances'. It opens with a riddle set by a king to the suitors for his daughter's hand and, as in numerous fairy tales, the penalty for failure is death. Pericles presents himself, and as soon as he hears the doggerel that has foxed so many of his predecessors, realizes to his horror what the answer is: that the king is living incestuously with the princess. Pericles flees the court, but the knowledge he has acquired is also fatal, his life is in jeopardy and his family's, too – or so it nearly turns out.

The name of the Sphinx is related to the verb for squeezing, as in English sphincter, and by extension, to throttling, so a thread of metaphors in the Oedipus myth connects the monster with

5 Jesse Prinz, Ara H. Merjian et al., *Revolt of the Sage* (London: Blain|Southern, 2017).

6 Marina Warner, *From the Beast to the Blonde*, pp.130–32.

7 Answer: Lot and his family (Exeter Riddle 44, translated by Craig Williamson).

the knotty structure of the riddle, with Jocasta, who commits suicide by hanging, and Myrrha, who dies after violating natural law against incest. The famous conundrum the Sphinx poses strangles her victims, tying them up in a knot of forbidden and mysterious relations.

The gods may break the taboo on incest (the Olympians are all siblings and all intermarried), and their divine avatars on earth, too (the pharaoh marries his sister), but ordinary humans transgress it to their peril. In Ovid's Metamorphoses, Myrrha falls passionately in love with her own father, and is abetted by her nurse to achieve her forbidden desire; she's then changed into a myrrh tree, whose name means bitterness, and her unborn baby is cut out of its trunk. This child of sorrow, Adonis, grows up to become beautiful, the beloved of Venus, is gored by a boar and himself turned into a flower – an anemone – after his violent death. Paloma Varga Weisz, one of the artists featured in the exhibition, is inspired by the strangeness-in-familiarity of such myths; her sculpture *Laszlo's dream* (p.39), presents a young boy, many-breasted like the Great Mother, Diana of Ephesus. This state of dreaming queerness returns with the eerie, prone *Somnambulist* (p.27), Cesare, from the film *The Cabinet of Dr. Caligari* (1920) is laid out in effigy next to the couch in Anna Freud's consulting room upstairs. The sculptor Daniel Silver also admits visitants from ambiguous dream narratives with his carved marble heads and figures, which appear to be classical or renaissance portraits but, as one looks, unsettle all expectations, as they dissolve and shift from recognizable or stable forms. Silver's cousin was the famous mannequin designer Adele Rootstein, who revolutionised shop window displays in the Sixties, and there seems to be a shared family taste for the uncanny simulacrum.

These motifs in *The Enigma of the Hour* – slippage between illusion and reality, dream visions, riddling formulae, and incestuous desire were all speaking to one another. It is striking that Linder is currently working on the subject of Myrrha.

fig.16

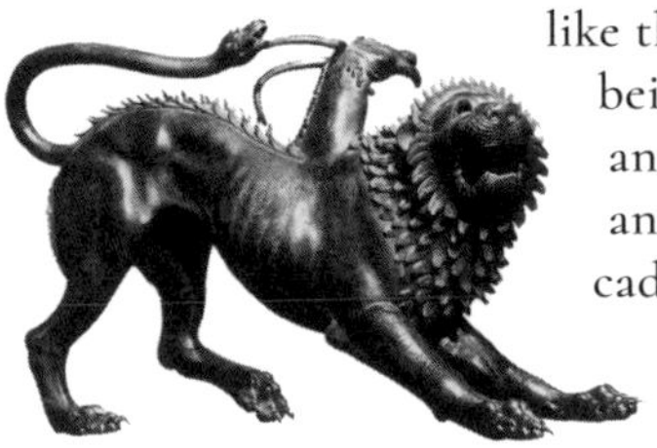

III Griffonage

Sir Thomas Browne, the Norfolk doctor, antiquarian and pioneering ethnographer, anticipates St Antony and Flaubert's concerns when he contemplates the existence of 'Poetical Animals', as he terms such creatures as the Sphinx. Gryphons or Griffins, he wrote, are among these lively products of human fantasy: 'if examined by the Doctrine of Animals, the invention is Monstrous, nor much inferior? unto the figment of Sphynx, Chimaera, and Harpies … though there be some flying Animals of mixed and participating Natures, that is, between Bird and quadruped … as Bats and some few others.'[8] He relates them to symbolic systems: [the Gryphon] was 'an Hieroglyphick of the Egyptians.'

A Griffin is a composite creature, like the Sphinx and the Chimaera, is a being made of diverse parts shuffled and assembled from different animals as in the Surrealist game cadavre exquis, or the English parlour game, of 'heads, bodies and tails'. For John Ruskin, a mythical hybrid could become, under the sign of the grotesque, perfectly beautiful. He decreed, in *Modern Painters*, that there exist 'True Griffins and False Griffins' – and he didn't mean that the true version's components must be correct and in the right order.[9] This seems an odd opinion about an entirely imaginary order of creature, but Ruskin was searching for a way of defining images that are ontologically coherent and experientially right: to distil the quintessence of griffon-ness. The arguments he put forward tend to be moral and their criteria are both hazy and antipathetic to contemporary

8 Sir Thomas Browne, *Pseudodoxia Epidemica III*, xi, (London: T.H. for E. Dod, 1646; 6th ed., 1672), pp. 142–44.

9 See e.g. http://www.artandpopularculture.com/True_and_False_Griffins; *True and False Griffins* is a drawing by John Ruskin, engraved by R.P. Cuff, from *Modern Painters* (Part IV. Of Many Things), first published in 1856. According to Ruskin, the left griffin is medieval and 'true', the right one classical and 'false'.

sensibilities: 'the vague and foolish inconsistencies of undisciplined dream or reverie may be mistaken for the compelled inconsistencies of thoughts too great to be well sustained, or clearly uttered. It is easy, I say, to understand what a difference there must indeed be between these; and yet how difficult it may be always to define it, or lay down laws for the discovery of it, except by the just instinct of minds set habitually in all things to discern right from wrong.'[10] Nevertheless, Ruskin diagnosed something fundamental, that a fantastic image, like the Chimaeras of Antony's visions or the apparitions in an analysand's nightmares, can feel like a success and deliver satisfaction when it convinces us that it has indeed brought its subject into existence: that the image reveals the character of a true griffin. Think of the white wolves sitting in the branches of a tree in that painting of the Wolf Man's dream. How memorably they recapture and transmit, in the material form of a haunting painting, his fascination and dread.

In relation to Freud, elements of enigma are found distributed between all three of these poetical and symbolic animals: the Sphinx sets a riddle, the Chimaera in her intrinsic nature cheats and eludes and baffles meaning, and the Griffin's name is related to gryph, or griph, and glyph, a word which means both mark, as in French *ma griffe* for signature, and signs communicating meaning, which demand decrypting, as with hieroglyphs. Such creatures are 'personified riddles who act as riddle masters', writes the scholar Eleanor Cook in her fascinating book, *Enigmas and Riddles in Literature*.[11] She riffs at length on the relationships between composite monsters and poetic tropes, which also assemble disparate elements to produce meaning. In *Alice's Adventures in Wonderland,* Lewis Carroll's Gryphon, with his partner the Mock Turtle, belong in a whole concatenation of enigmatic figures who explain something to Alice in ways that leave her more puzzled than before. As in the dreamwork, plays on words matter towards making meaning interpretation. The Gryphon tells Alice,

> *"I went to the Classical master... he was an old crab, he was."*
>
> *"I never went to him," the Mock Turtle said with a sigh. "He taught Laughing and Grief, they used to say."*[12]

Here the sound play on 'Latin and Greek' reflects the principle that Freud explores, that jokes express resistance to despair, while the pun on Grief widens to include Gryph: 'For what else is a laughing grief but a *griph* (pronounced *grief*, as in the first syllable of *griphos*), and how odd that the root of the Greek word for a joking riddle should sound the same as the English word for sorrow.'[13] As Eleanor Cook, observes, Lewis Carroll's famous book offers us 'something like a topography of enigma, including griph'.[14] Wonderland is a Theban desert, packed with puzzling encounters, and many riddling uses of language, including punning jokes, as the child questor confronts mysterious monsters and situations and tries to understand them.

The famous oracles of antiquity record punning messages which, as in the sphinx's puzzle, the Gryphon's jokes, and dreams, yield a patent sense which misleads the petitioner, often lulling them into a false sense of security, then proves true: at Delphi, a Scythian prince was told by the Pythia to beware of a mouse (*mus*), and so he mercilessly had all mice exterminated and banned anyone called Mus from his presence, but eventually had an infected arm and died of sepsis in the muscle (also *mus*).[15] Similarly, when Croesus, the fabulously rich King of Lydia, consulted the oracle on whether he should go to war with

10 *Ibid.*

11 Eleanor Cook, *Enigmas and Riddles in Literature* (Cambridge: Cambridge University Press, 2006), p.166.

12 Lewis Carroll, and Hugh Haughton (ed.), *Alice's Adventures in Wonderland and Through the Looking-Glass* (London: Penguin, 1998), p.85.

13 Cook, *Enigmas and Riddles in Literature*, p.161.

14 *Ibid.*, p.160.

15 See Eloise Hart, 'The Delphic Oracle', in *Sunrise* (October/November 1985).

the Persian, he was delighted to hear that he would destroy a great empire. He did not understand that it was his own power the prophetess had in mind.

Myths of this antiquity hide their meanings in plain sight, another form of epiphany central to Freud's hermeneutics.

Simon Moretti inhabits the English language with an acute ear for its ambiguities. He delights in mishearings – Misreadings, as he calls them – and the messages they bring, inadvertently. They're inadvertent riddles, and the list he has made shows they're also 'locutions' – acoustic visions, like Joan of Arc's voices, which she said, 'came in the name of the light'. His misreadings include poetic, pregnant thoughts fraught with surreal overtones: 'a cup in the ocean', 'zero, a faraway song', 'pale sight', 'splendour in the glass', 'like the fire in the egg', 'clockworks dreamwork' 'the fiction of time', 'fantasmarama', 'atonement with the feather', 'smoking poems' – phrases which, falling athwart conventional parlance, connect suggestively to *The Enigma of the Hour* and its perspective on psychoanalysis. Another of these earwitnesses, to borrow a wonderfully rich made-up word of Elias Canetti's,[16] gives Simon Moretti the text for the neon piece hung above the famous couch: 'only day and night' (p.20).

In his own works, Moretti juxtaposes found images, some magnified, others inverted, and creates unexpected conjunctions of scale and enigmatic relations. His collages quarry stills from films that enthral him and remain enigmas: *Untitled (Oedipus Rex/ The Infernal Machine) #1* (p.45) includes the immortally beautiful Silvana Mangano cradling her husband-son in the her lap from Pasolini's 1967 masterpiece *Oedipus Rex*; *Untitled (Oedipus Rex/The Infernal Machine) #2* (p.47) includes another diva, Jeanne Moreau, in a blonde Egyptian wig, and shows the Sphinx as an African mask, as a monstrous Magna Mater, legs akimbo, birthing unnameable mysteries from a cave under a cliff.

16 Canetti Earwitness.

These collages share qualities of playful allusiveness and sumptuous glamour with the works of Linder. Both artists revel in the mysterious detonations of sensation that chance encounters set off: Linder superimposes the involution of a shell in the place of a woman's head, to uncanny, lovely effect. Technically collages, these images edge towards the hieroglyph and the rebus, but their opacity resists easy answers: these are riddles without a solution (as is the case with many ancient riddles from the Exeter book). You could call them griffonages. Their mystery compels you to look, and the way they resist decipherment, inspires pleasure in the viewer. This aesthetic effect on us does not depend on understanding what an image means but enjoying its perplexity.

fig.17

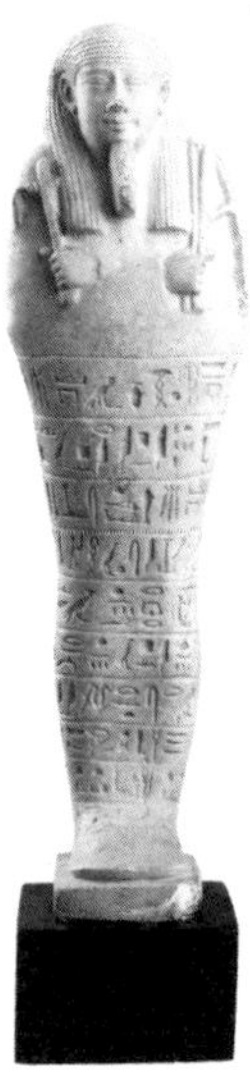

The psychoanalytic method proceeds as code-breaking does, as the doctor reads dream symbols, seeing beneath appearances to the encrypted story they enclose. Many of the statuettes and images Freud collected are recognisable figures of individual beings (Eros, Athena, Thoth the baboon scribe of the Egyptian pantheon). But many items in his cabinet and on his table and surrounding shelves in the consulting room are symbolic figures, and he gave his inner circle rings set with gems incised with ciphers – enigmas for a group that was itself secret. The devices and emblems, dating from far distant antiquity as well as the Renaissance and later, cast the wearer in the role of a master of hidden meaning.

But the Sphinx's riddle clearly points to the inevitable march of time in every single life, and by extension, in the unfolding of whole civilisations. Freud often deploys, as an interpretive tool, archaeological resonances between the psyche and culture and history, between the childhood of an individual, the depths of the unconscious and the deep time of culture at the beginning. The antiquities he collected, from ancient Egypt and Ancient Greece correspond to this model he found so fruitful. The psychoanalytic hour explores the analysand's psyche by obeying the riddle, and going back into the past, into the infancy – that first crawling on all fours – and building towards the future.

IV The Questioner and the Answerer

The Enigma of the Hour returns us to the dynamics of that scene in the Theban desert from so long ago. Yet, in Ingres's monumental painting (p.4), the roles of Oedipus and the Sphinx seem reversed, the man appearing to be asking her a question rather than submitting himself to her test. His crooked finger traditionally expresses leadership: John the Baptist points the way to Jesus. It also seems to be eliciting a response from the Monster, beckoning to her to be more forthcoming. Is Oedipus answering the Sphinx or looking to her wisdom to answer questions of his own? Is the Sphinx a conduit of greater knowledge from a source beyond her moment of power? The Journal's device represents the Sphinx, who set the original riddle, as herself a riddle that he is confronting. Oedipus becomes both the subject and the object of inquiry, and the Sphinx an oracle he is consulting, as well as a mystery to solve. She speaks wisdom that is greater than herself, just as the Pythia at Delphi was inspired to make her pronouncements by the god of prophecy, Apollo, in whose temple she served. The famous instruction, 'Know Thyself', was carved on the lintel of the temple at Delphi. It was the reply Apollo gave, through his prophetess, to the question put to him by Chilon of Sparta, 'What is best for man?' Oedipus seems to be asking the Sphinx the same question.

The mise-en-scene of the analytic couch similarly blurs distinction between questioner and answerer as the analysand searches for self-knowledge. Freud seated himself behind the head of the couch, out of sight, as he listened to the messages from his patient, receiving them in near silence; the task of interpreting, correctly, their coded contents then fell to him.

fig. 18

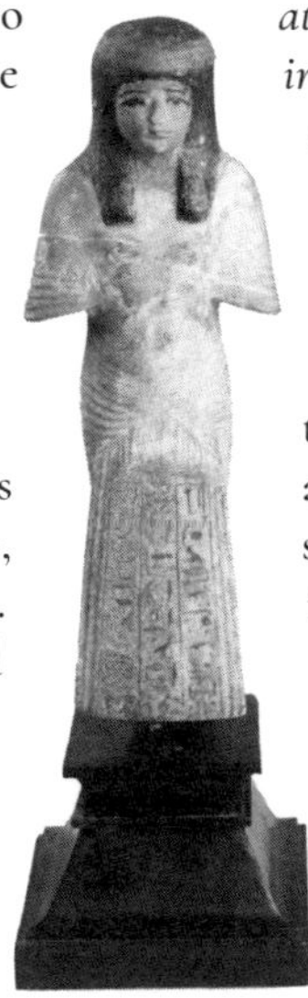

In several respects he takes on the role of the *shabti*, another Egyptian figure who features in Freud's collection. Shabti were found in great numbers in tombs, some of them made of turquoise frit, others in glazed terracotta, as with Freud's examples; they are upright figures who were buried with the dead man or woman to work ceaselessly on their behalf. For in the Egyptian afterlife, routine household tasks continued, and so the wealthy forestalled labour ahead by installing surrogates to perform for them, while they lay at rest. Shabti are often inscribed with a spell:

> *"Here I am" you shall say when you are called at any time to serve, to cultivate the fields, to irrigate the channels, to transport by boat the sand of the east to the west and vice-versa. "Here I am" you shall say.*[17]

Their name means, Answerer, and they are the doppelgangers of the dead; they also resemble the self whom we see, apparently autonomous, in a dream, and the subject summoned to shared consciousness in the analytic process; this substitute's relation to the dead also reproduces the reciprocal relations it is necessary to establish between the subject who speaks and the oracle who listens and tries to interpret what is being asked. Oracles involve both parties, and the meanings are missed – and made – together. Curators answer the questions posed by the subjects of a show; they are the answering shabti who are acting on behalf of artists and writers to make meanings appear.

17 Shabti spell, Egyptian collection, Ashmolean Museum, Oxford.

fig. 15 *Figure of Sphinx*, Southern Italian, late 5th to early 4th century BC. Museum no. 4387. Collection of the Freud Museum London.

fig. 16 *Chimera of Arezzo*, 5th century BC, Bronze.

fig. 17 *Shabti Figure of Djehutyemheb*, Egyptian, New Kingdom (late 18th-18th Dynasty). Museum no. 3269. Collection of the Freud Museum London.

fig. 18 *Shabti statuette*, Egyptian, Late Period. Museum no. 3463. Collection of the Freud Museum London.

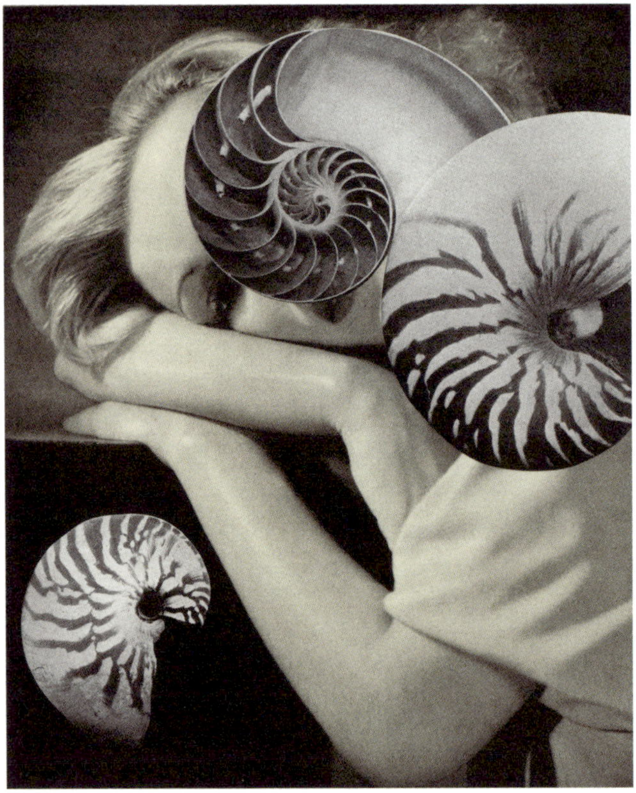

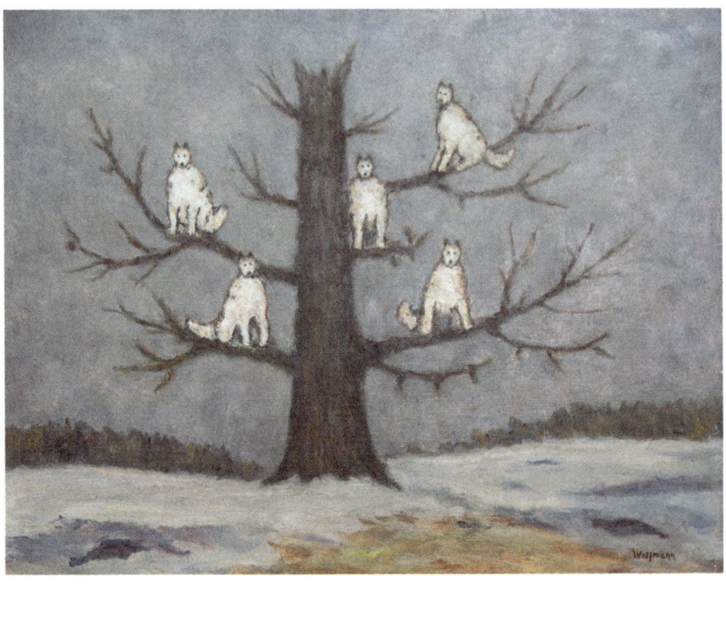

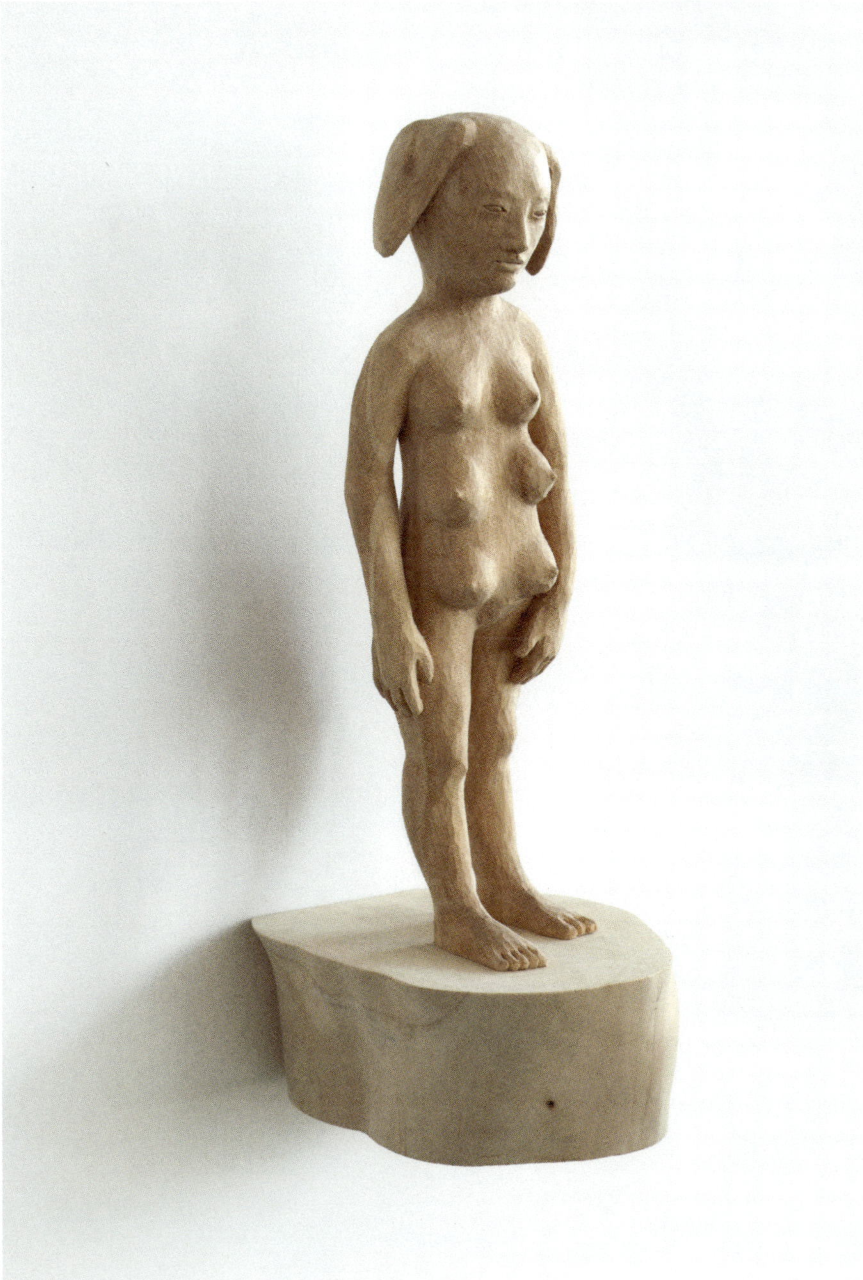

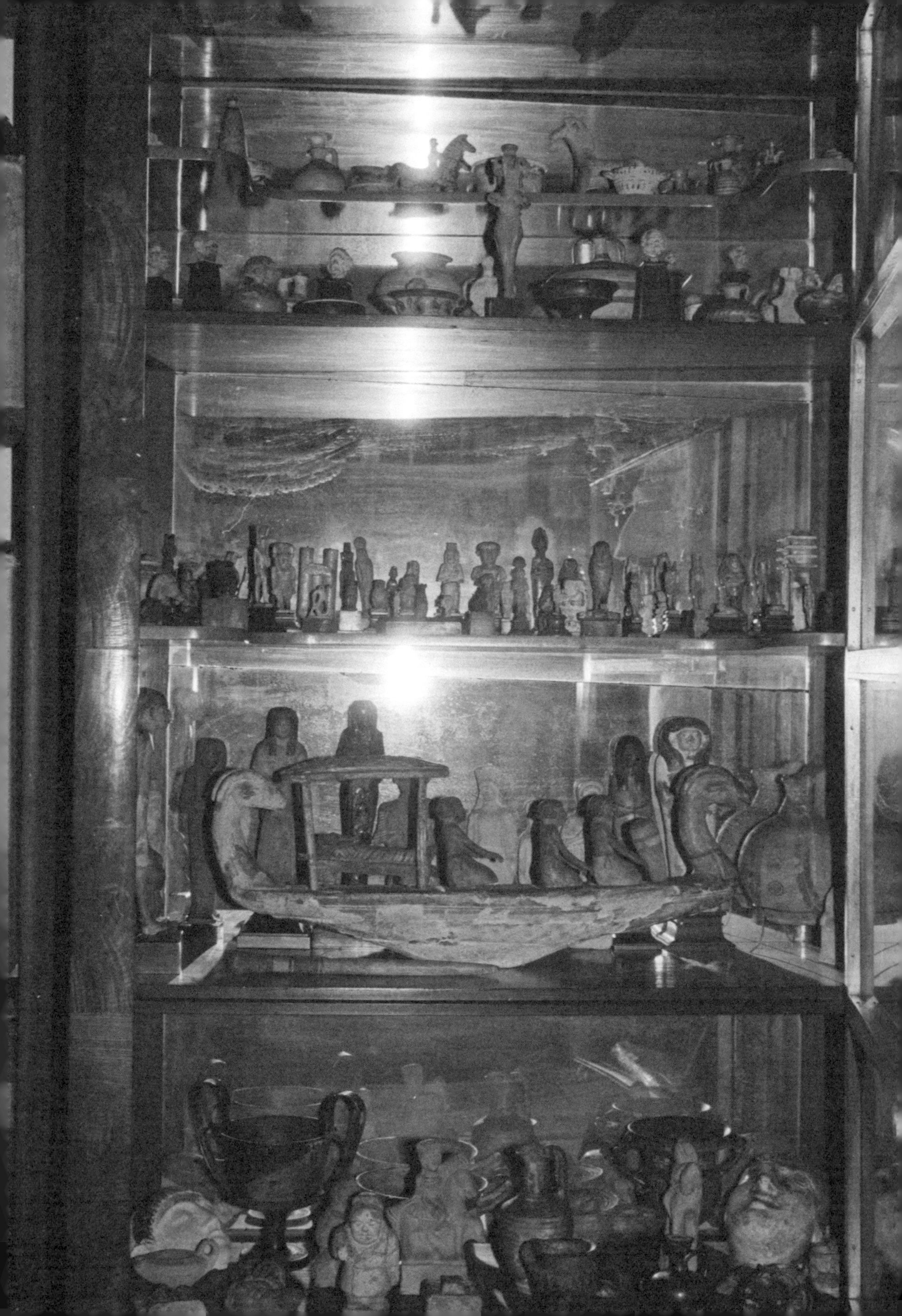

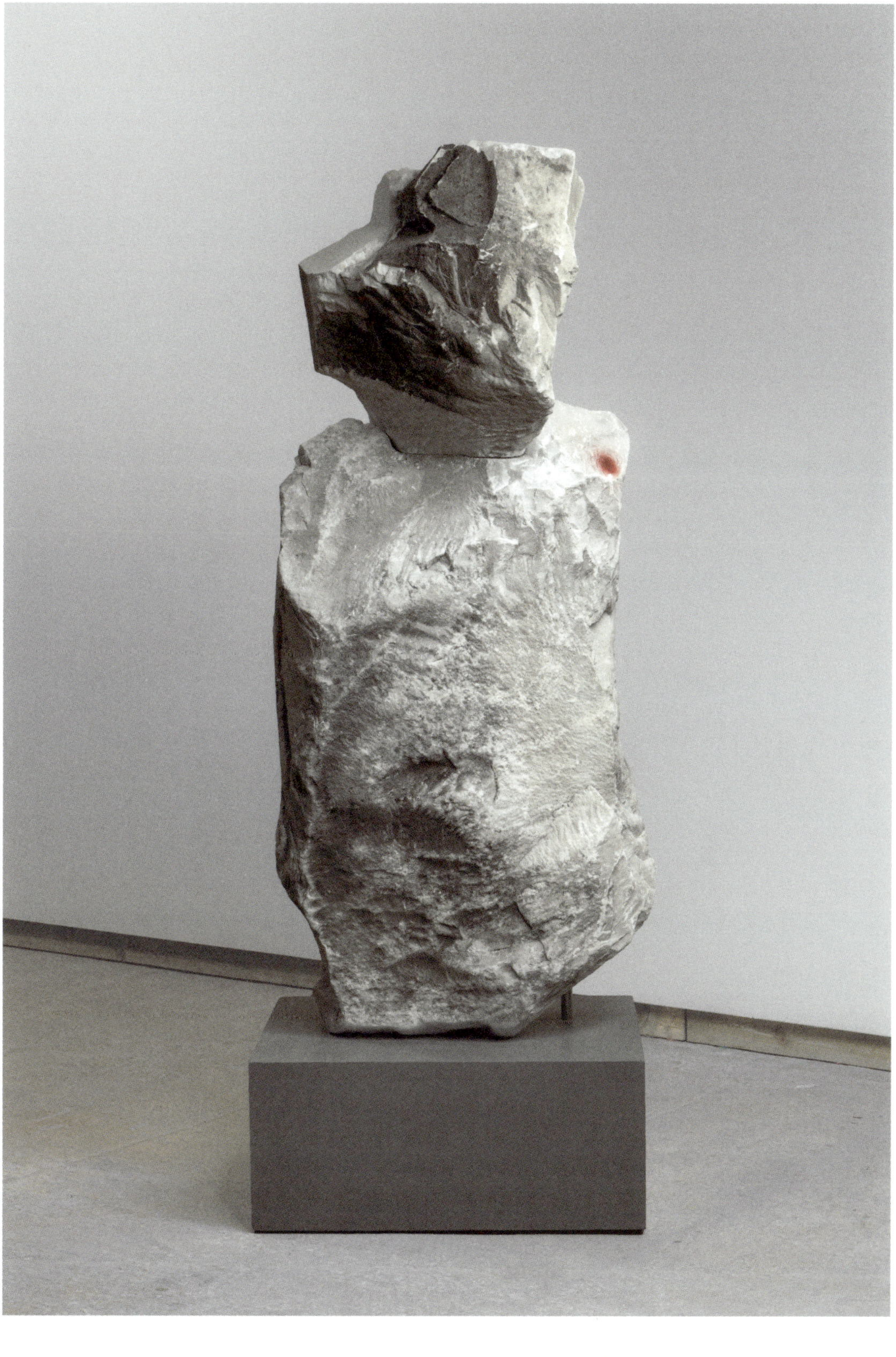

we shall have to confess that the features of dream-life which we have considered hitherto, and which have been ascribed to its detachment from the external world, do not account completely for its strange character …

after waking, we reproduce a dream from memory; but, whether we succeed in making this re-translation wholly or only in part, the dream remains no less enigmatic than before.

we cannot dismiss the probability that in dreams too the transformation of thoughts into visual images may be in part the result of the attraction which memories couched in visual form and eager for revival bring to bear upon thoughts cut off from consciousness and struggling to find expression

– Sigmund Freud, *The Interpretation of Dreams* (1900)

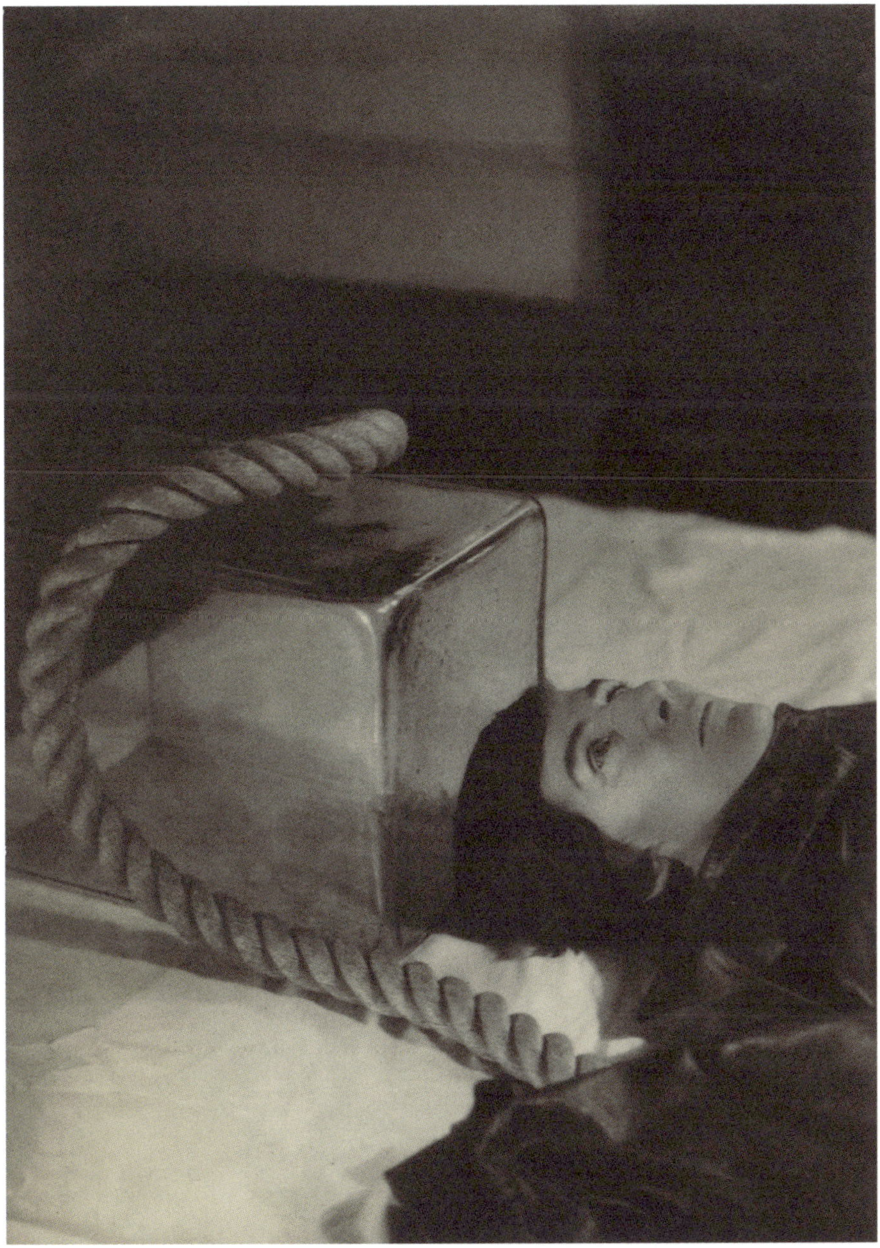

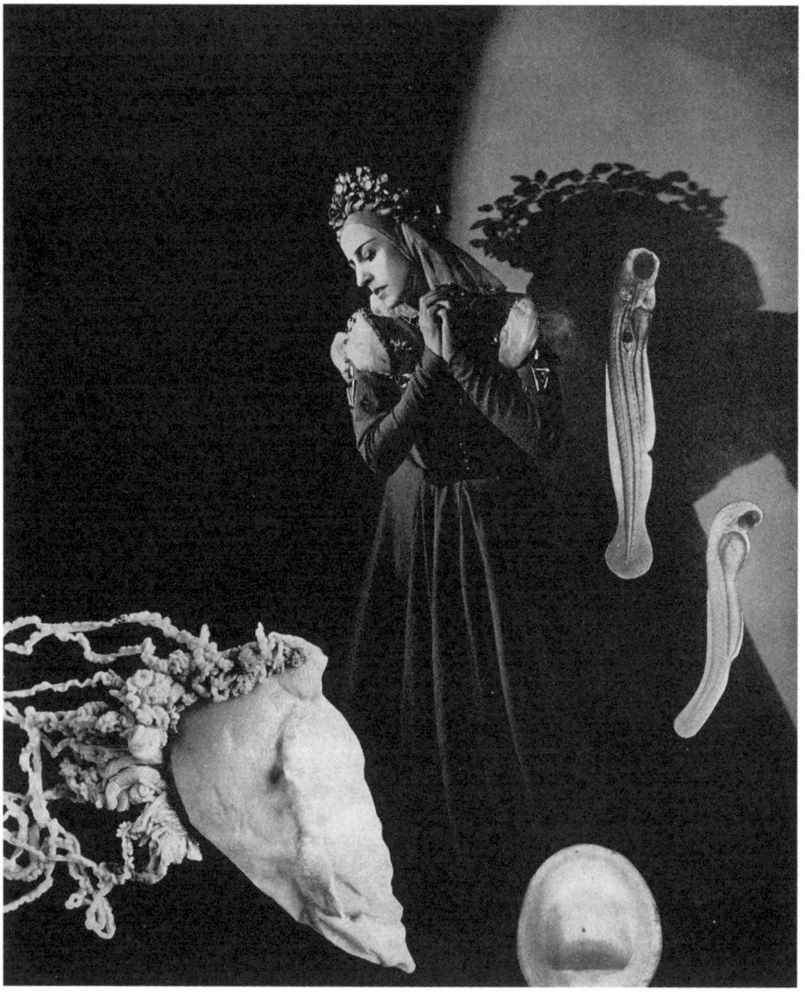

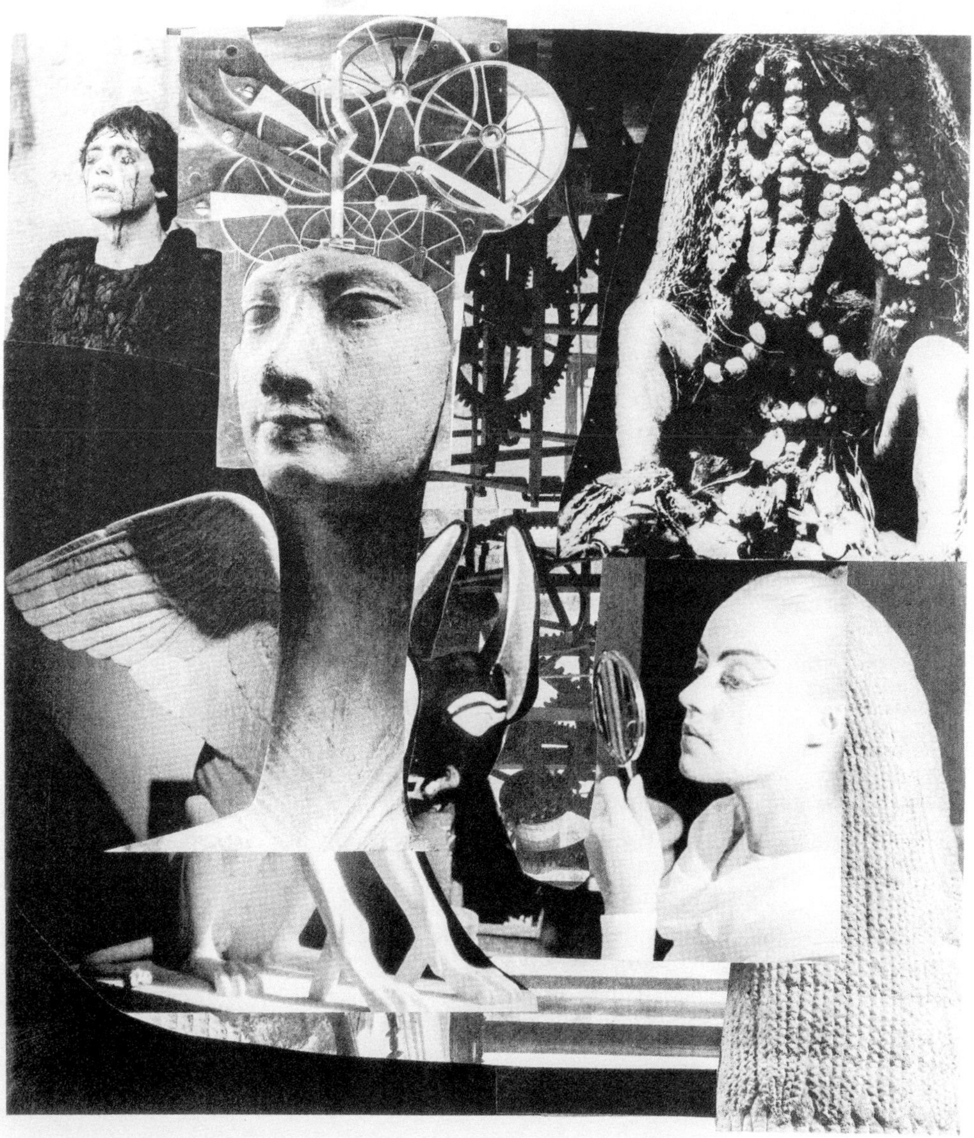

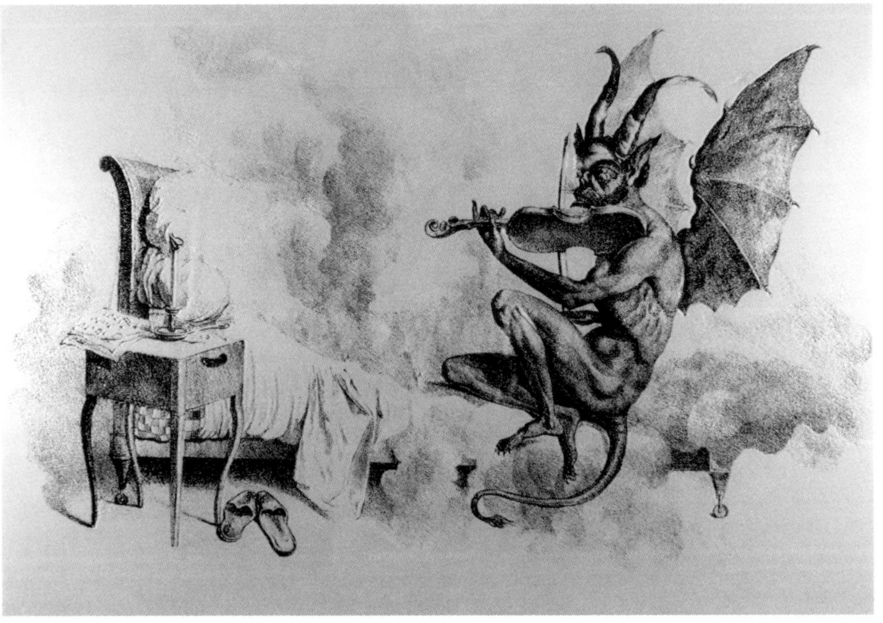

The 'creative' imagination, indeed, is quite incapable of inventing anything; it can only combine components that are strange to one another … The material offered to the dream-work consists of thoughts – a few of which may be objectionable and unacceptable, but which are correctly constructed and expressed. The dream-work puts these thoughts into another form, and it is a strange and incomprehensible fact that in making this translation (this rendering, as it were, into another script or language) these methods of merging or combining are brought into use.

– Sigmund Freud, *Introductory Lectures on Psycho-Analysis* (1916)

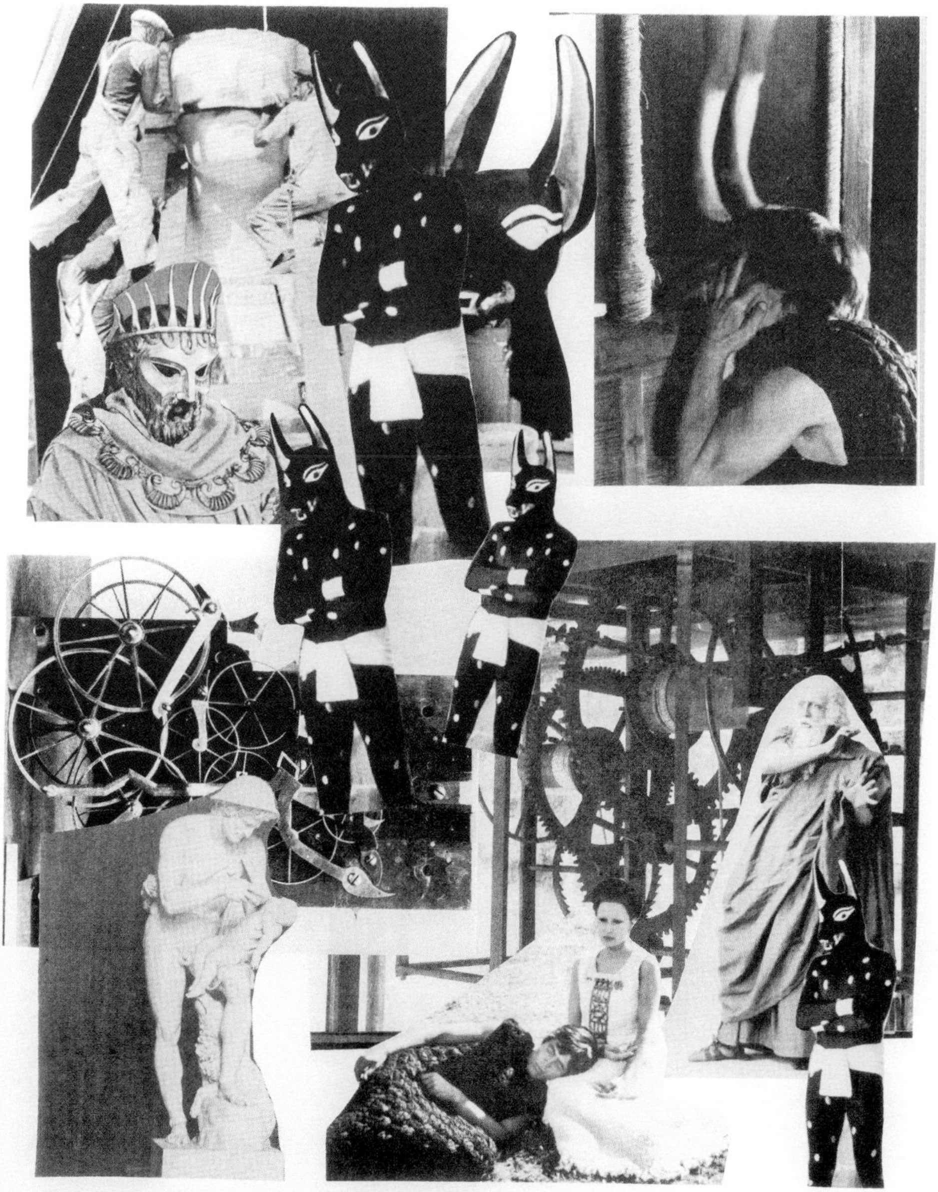

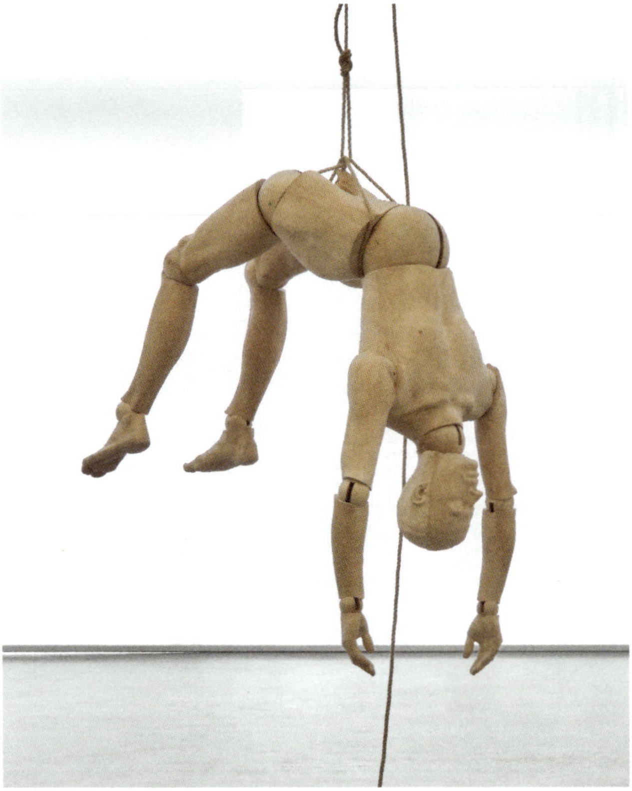

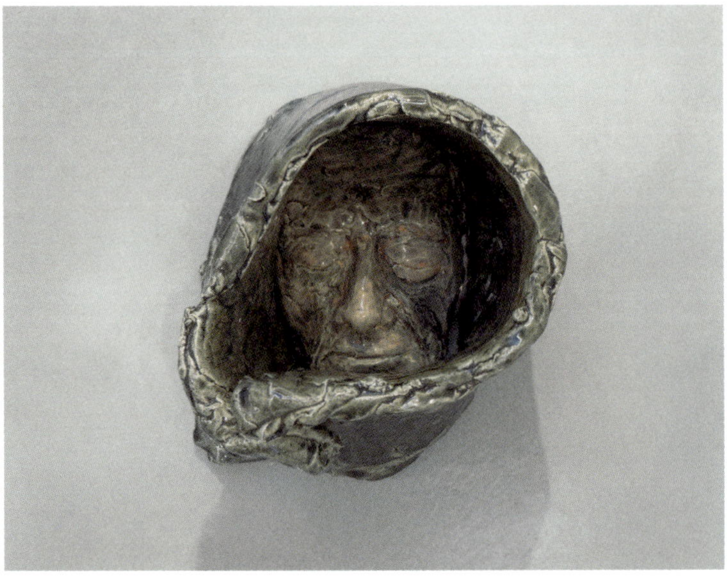

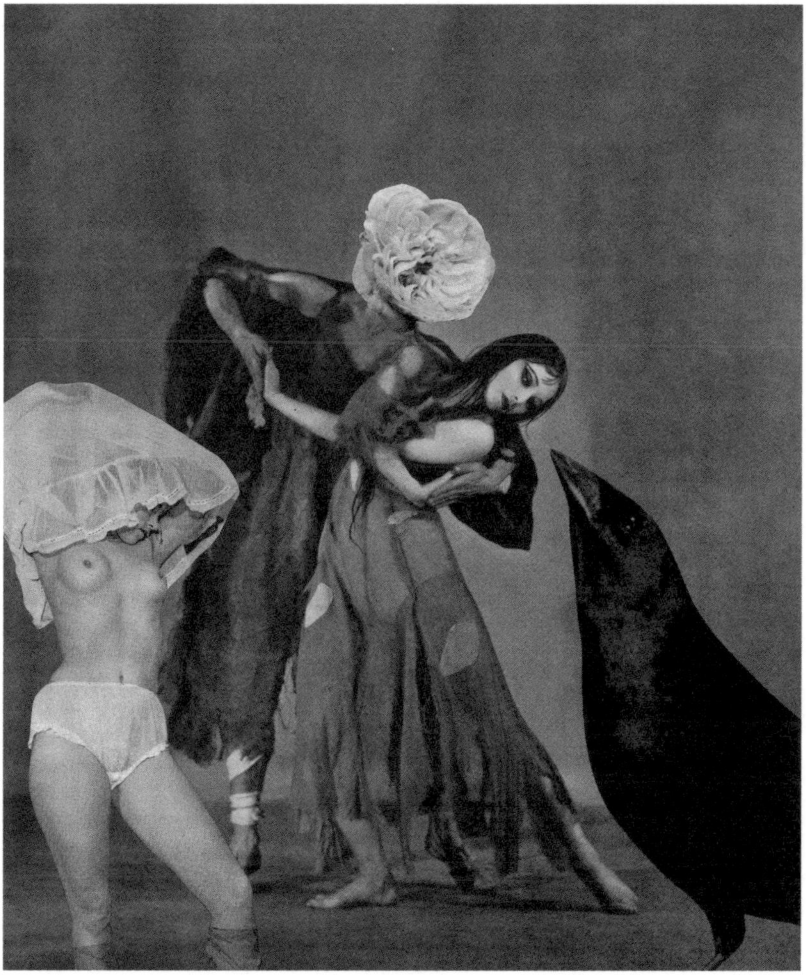

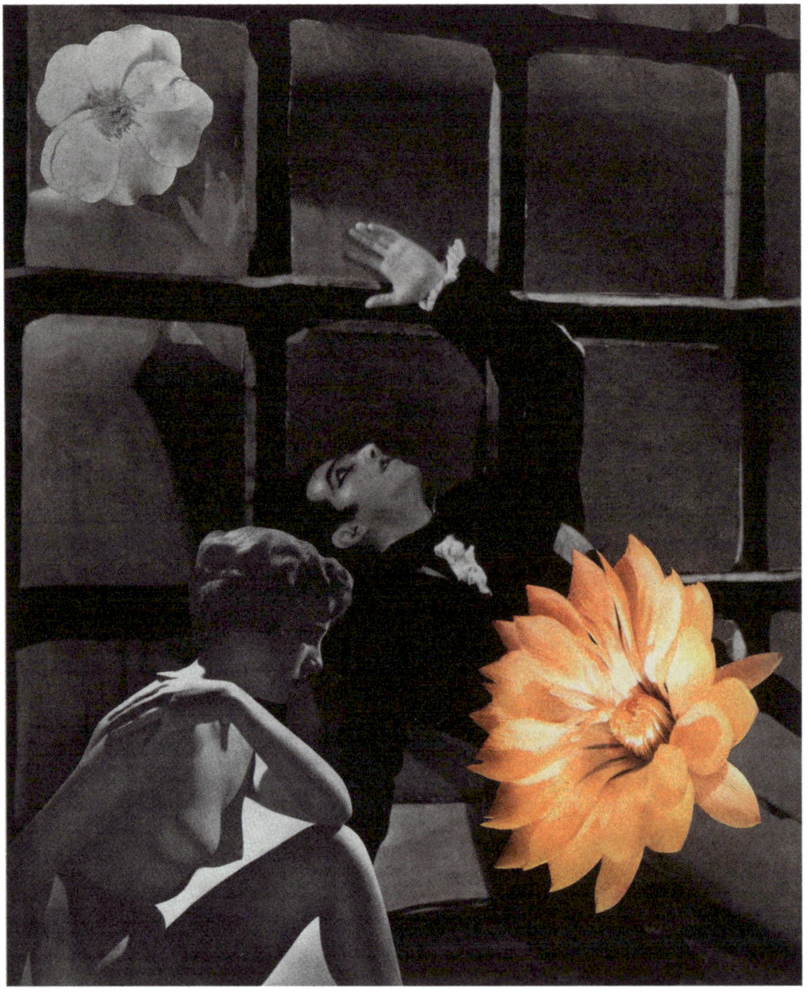

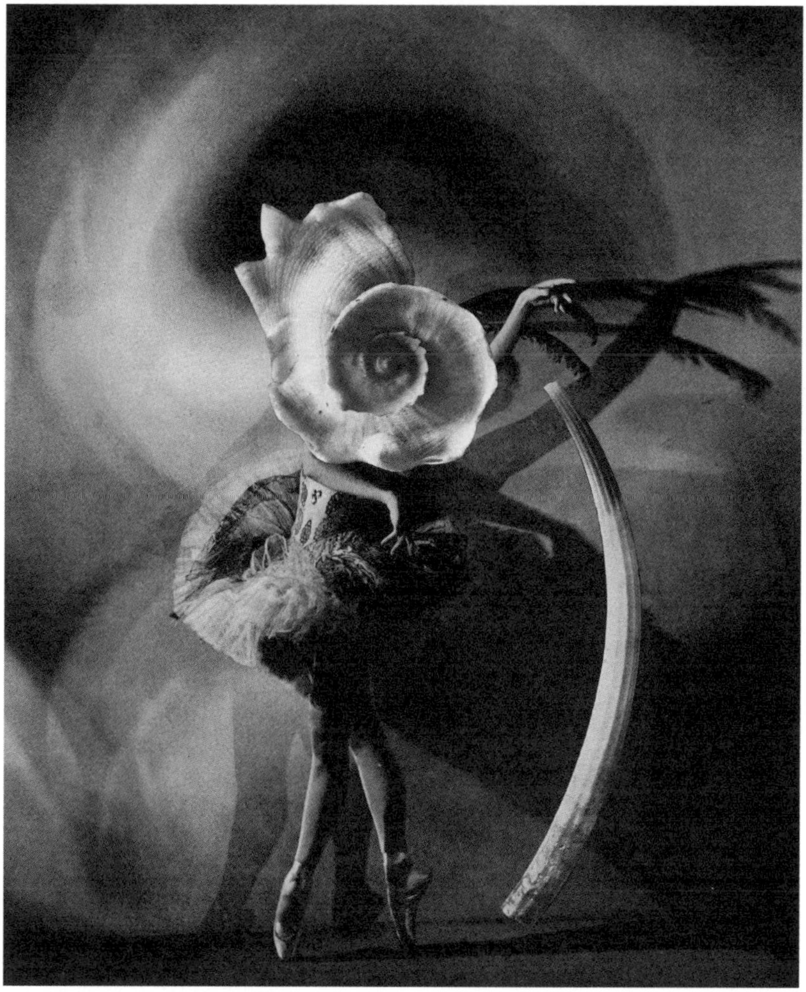

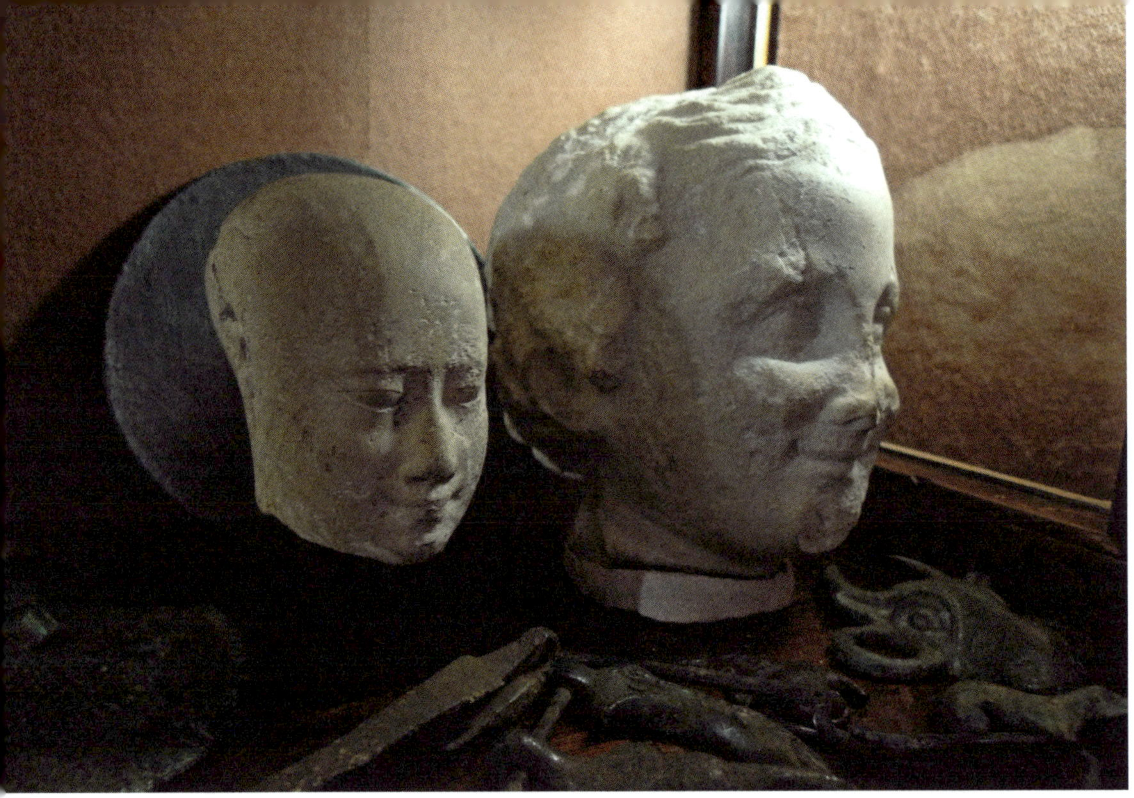

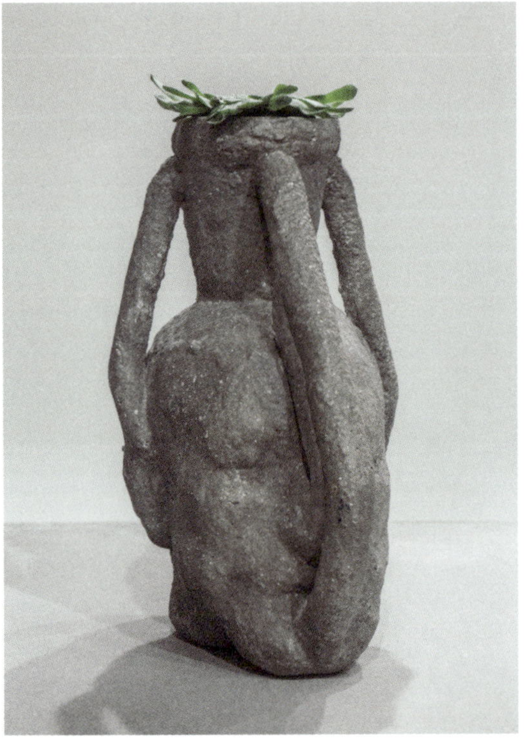

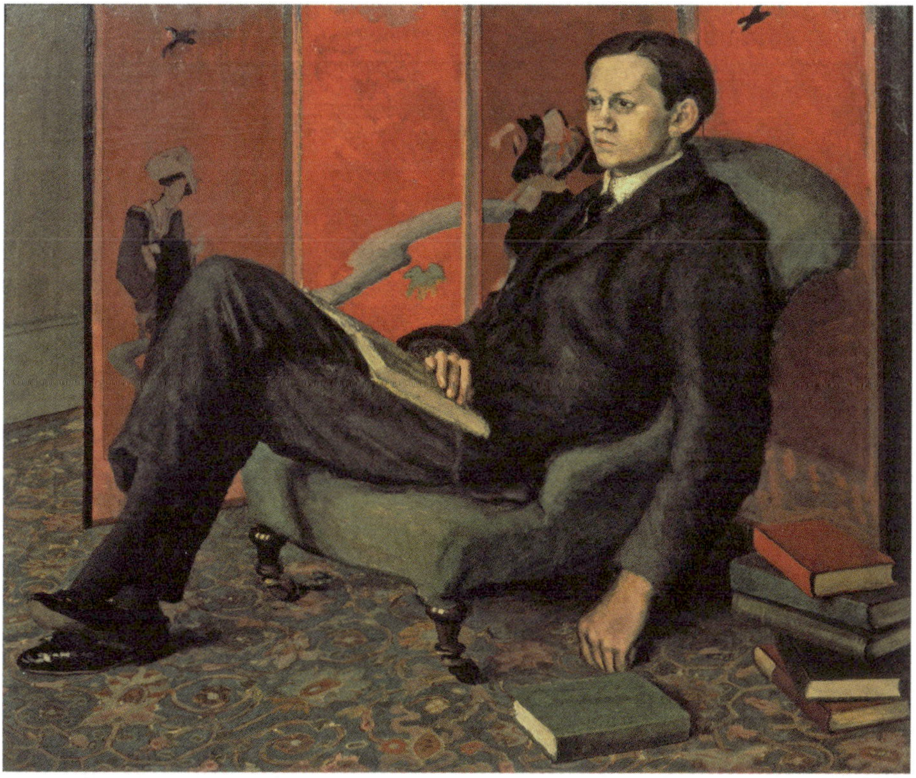

DREAMLAND AND SOMNAMBULISM

[Vol.III.No.4, January, 1882]

[*To the Editor.*

(1) ARE dreams always real? If so, what produces them?
Yours most fraternally and obediently,
JEHANGIR CURSETJI TARACHAND]

In dreaming, or in somnambulism, the brain is asleep only in parts, and is called into action through the agency of the external senses, owing to some peculiar cause; a word pronounced, a thought, or picture lingering dormant in one of the cells of memory, and awakened by a sudden noise, the fall of a stone, suggesting instantaneously to this half-dreamy fancy of the sleeper walls of masonry, and so on. When one is suddenly startled in his sleep without becoming fully awake, he does not begin and terminate his dream with the simple noise which partially awoke him, but often experiences in his dream a long train of events concentrated within the brief space of time the sound occupies, and to be attributed solely to that sound. Generally dreams are induced by the waking associations which precede them. Some of them produce such an impression that the slightest idea in the direction of any subject associated with a particular dream may bring its recurrence years after.

Somnambulism, premonitions and second sight are but a disposition, whether accidental or habitual, to dream, awake, or during a voluntary, self-induced, or yet natural sleep; *i.e.*, to perceive [and guess by intuition] the analogical reflections of the astral light...

H.P. Blavatsky

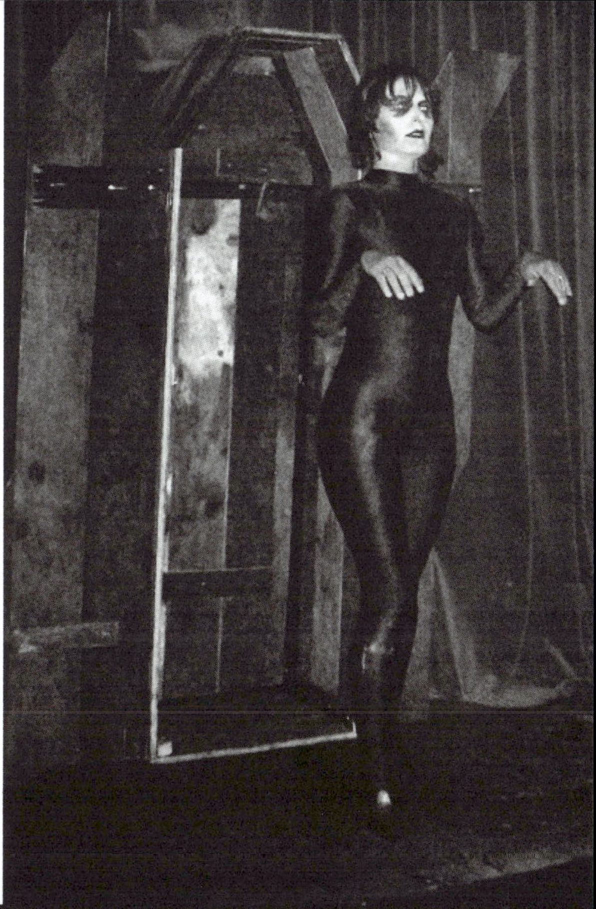
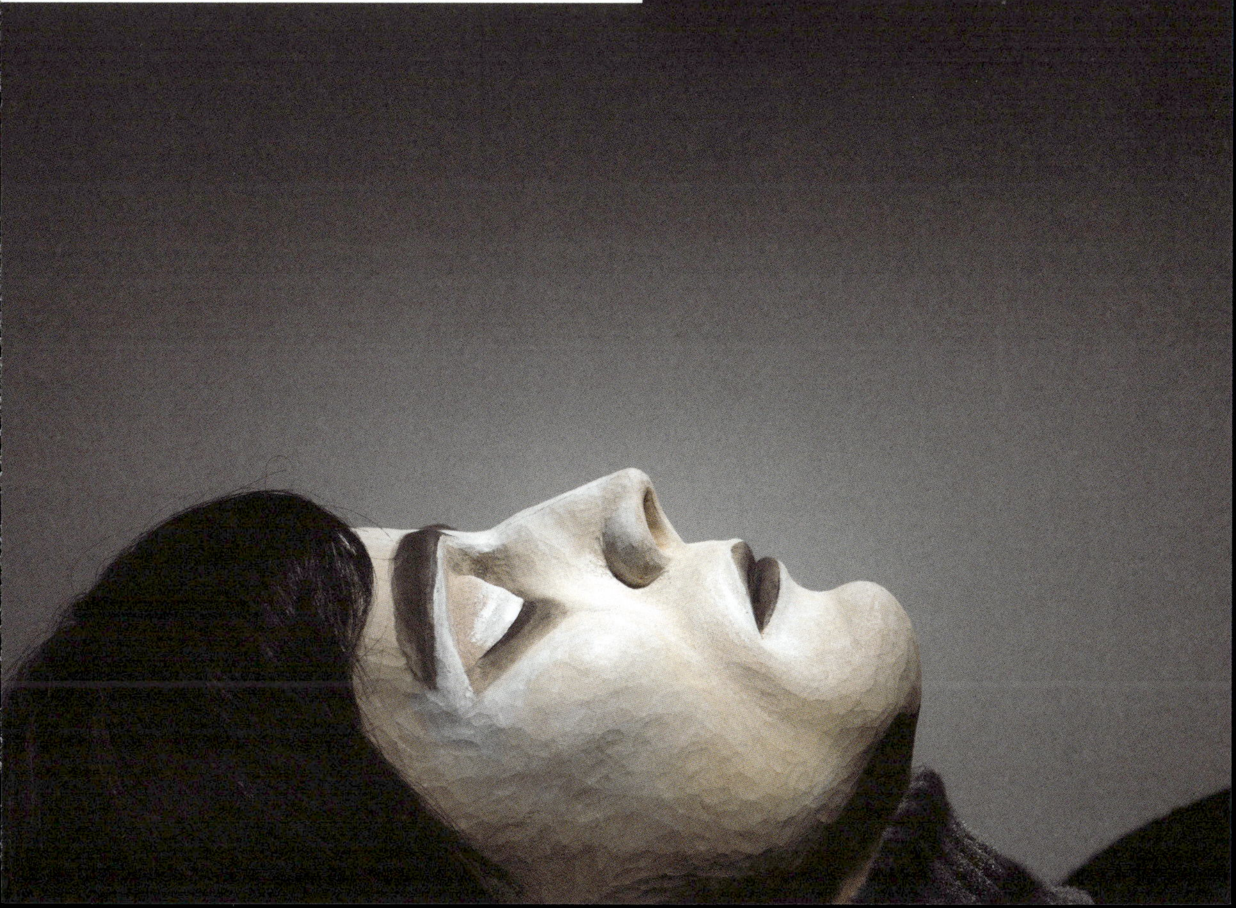

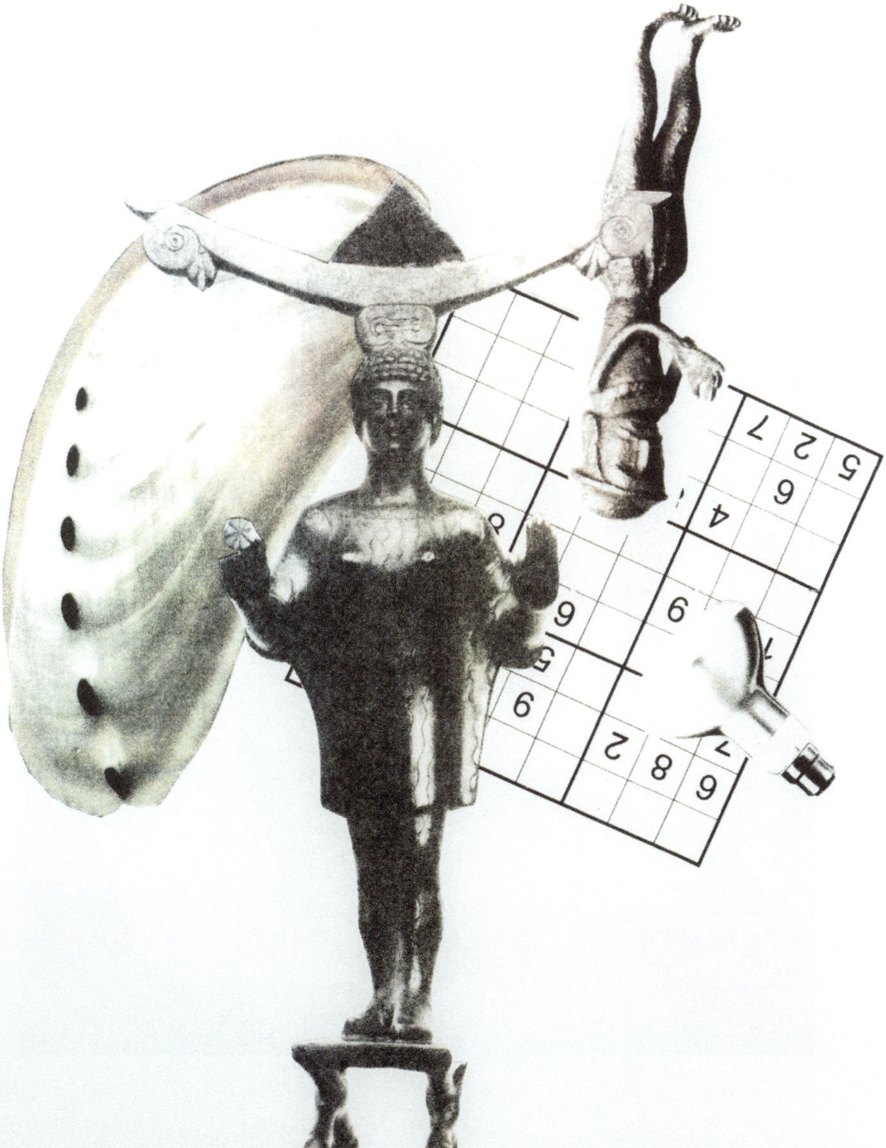

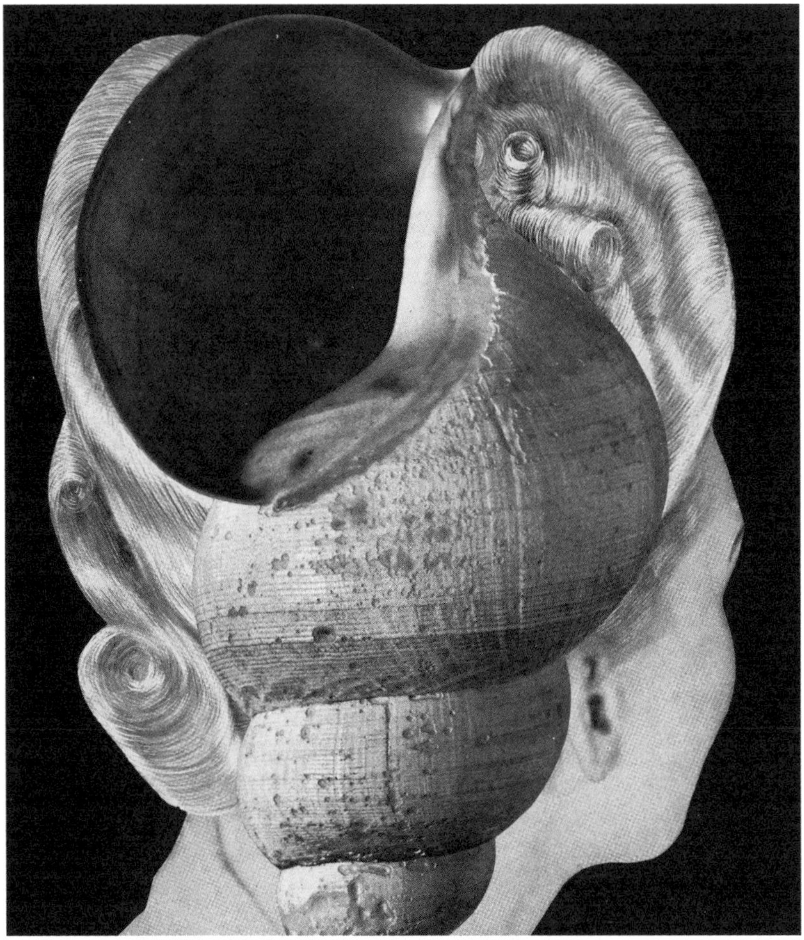

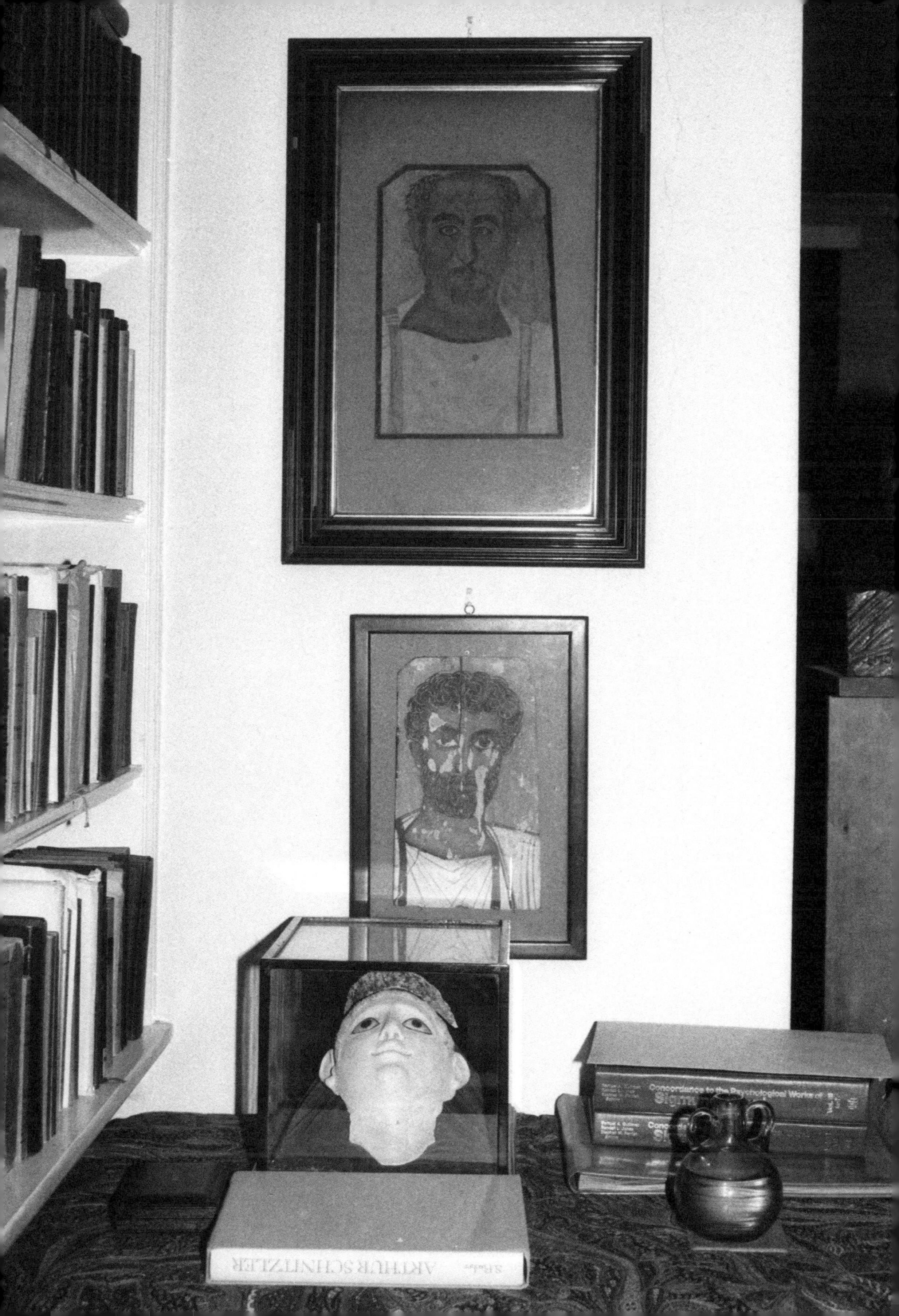
Concordance to the Psychological Works of
ARTHUR SCHNITZLER

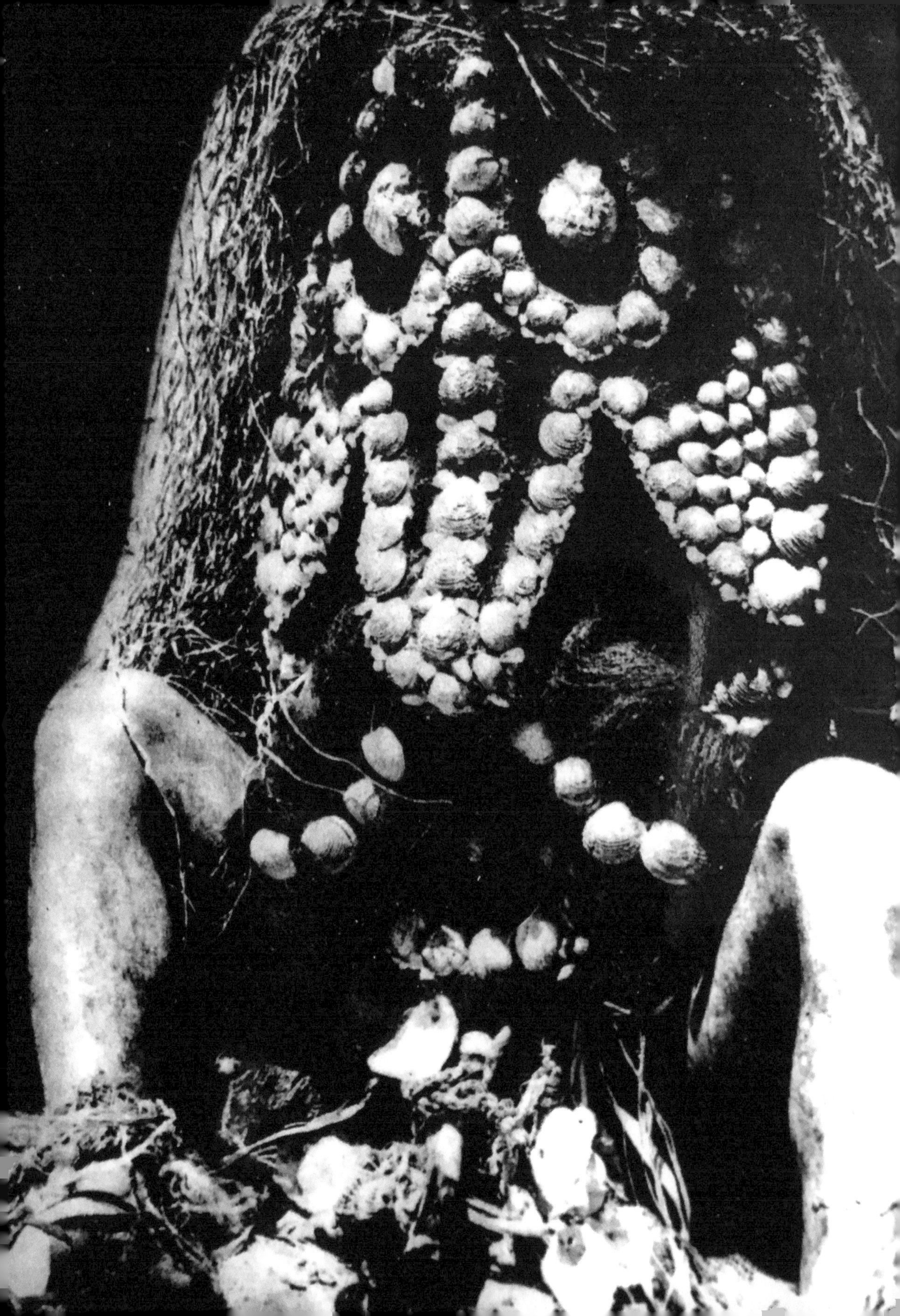

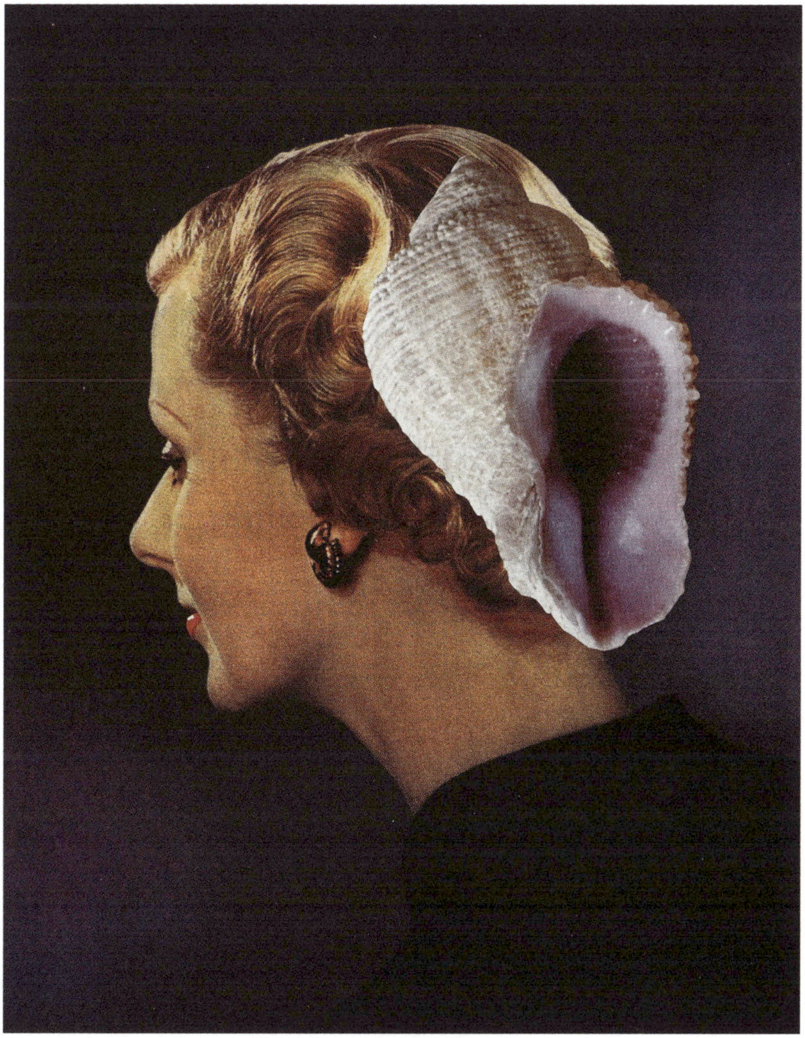

Fix on Oedipus your eyes,
Who resolved the dark enigma, noblest champion and most wise.
Like a star his envied fortune mounted beaming far and wide:
Now he sinks in seas of anguish, whelmed beneath a raging tide…

– Sophocles, *Oedipus Rex*

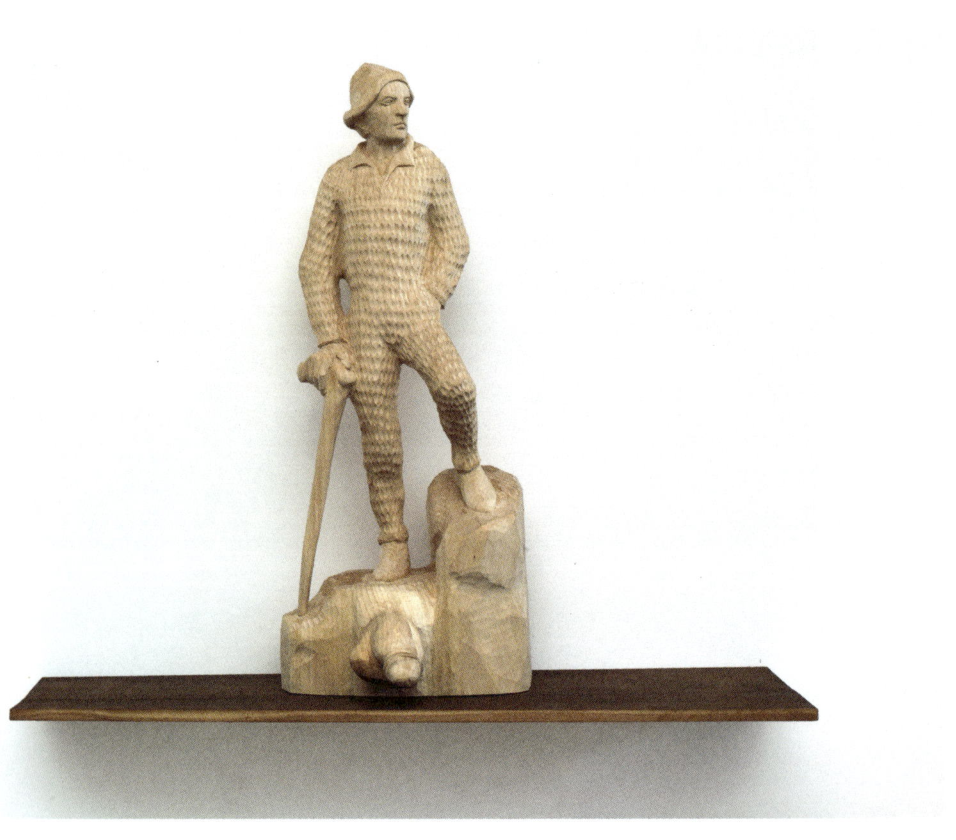

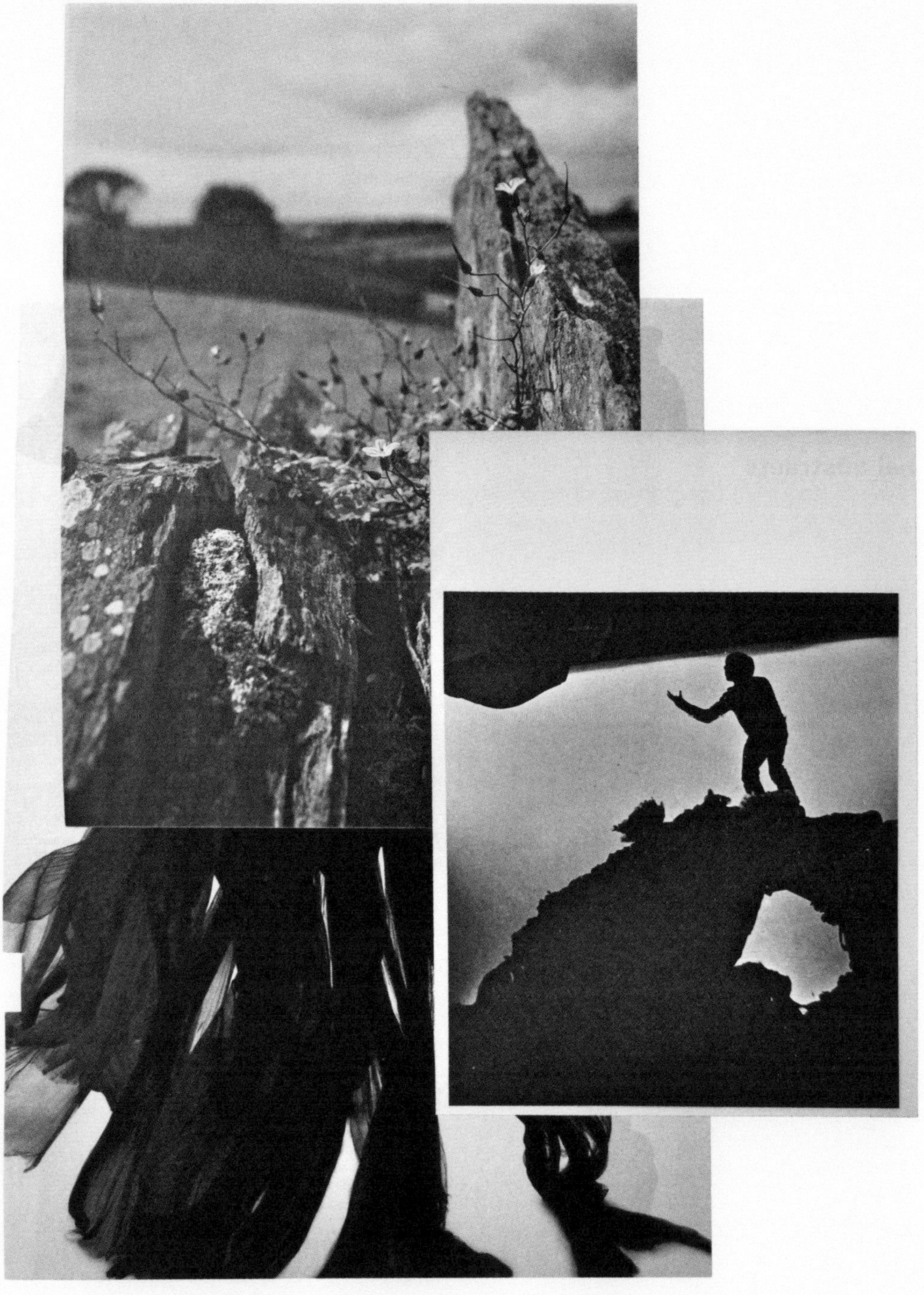

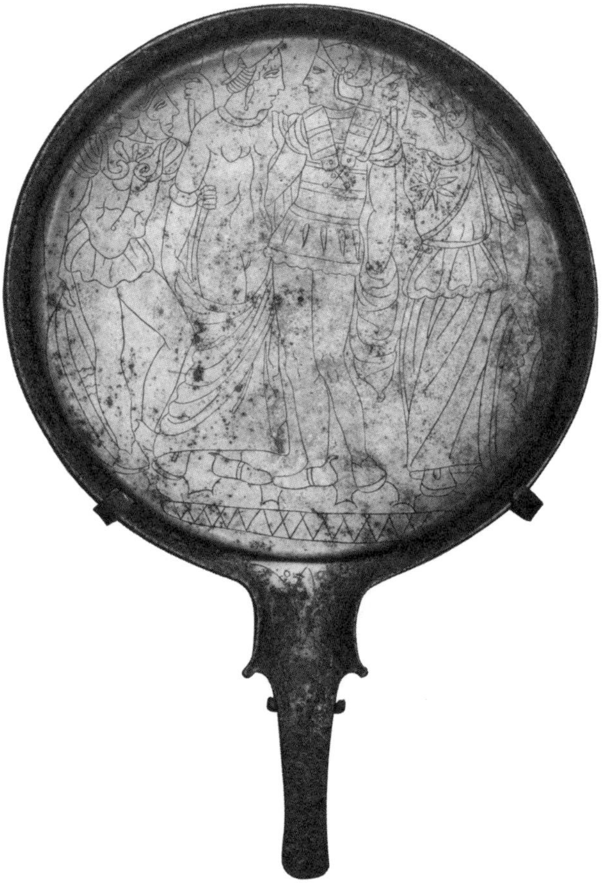

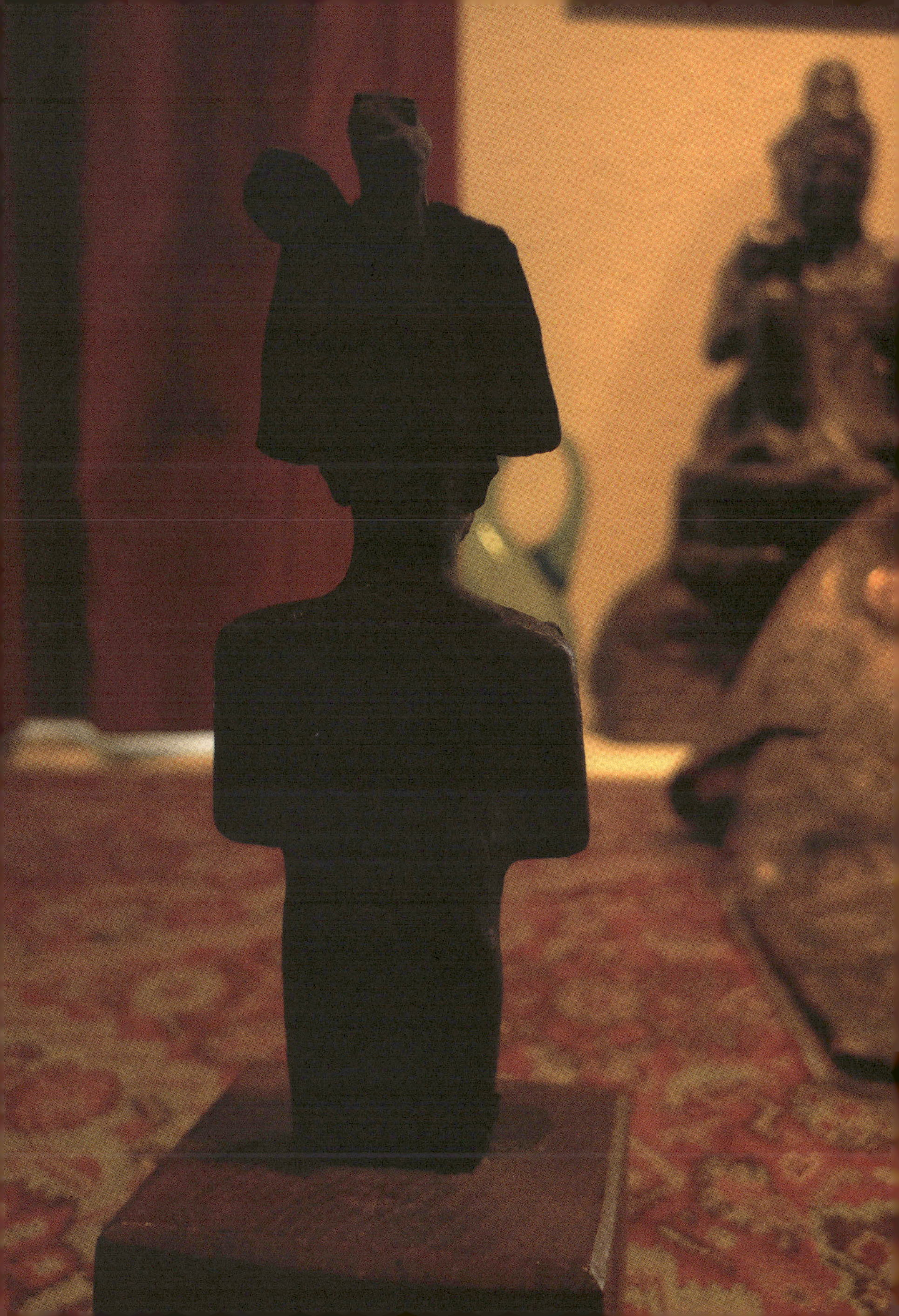

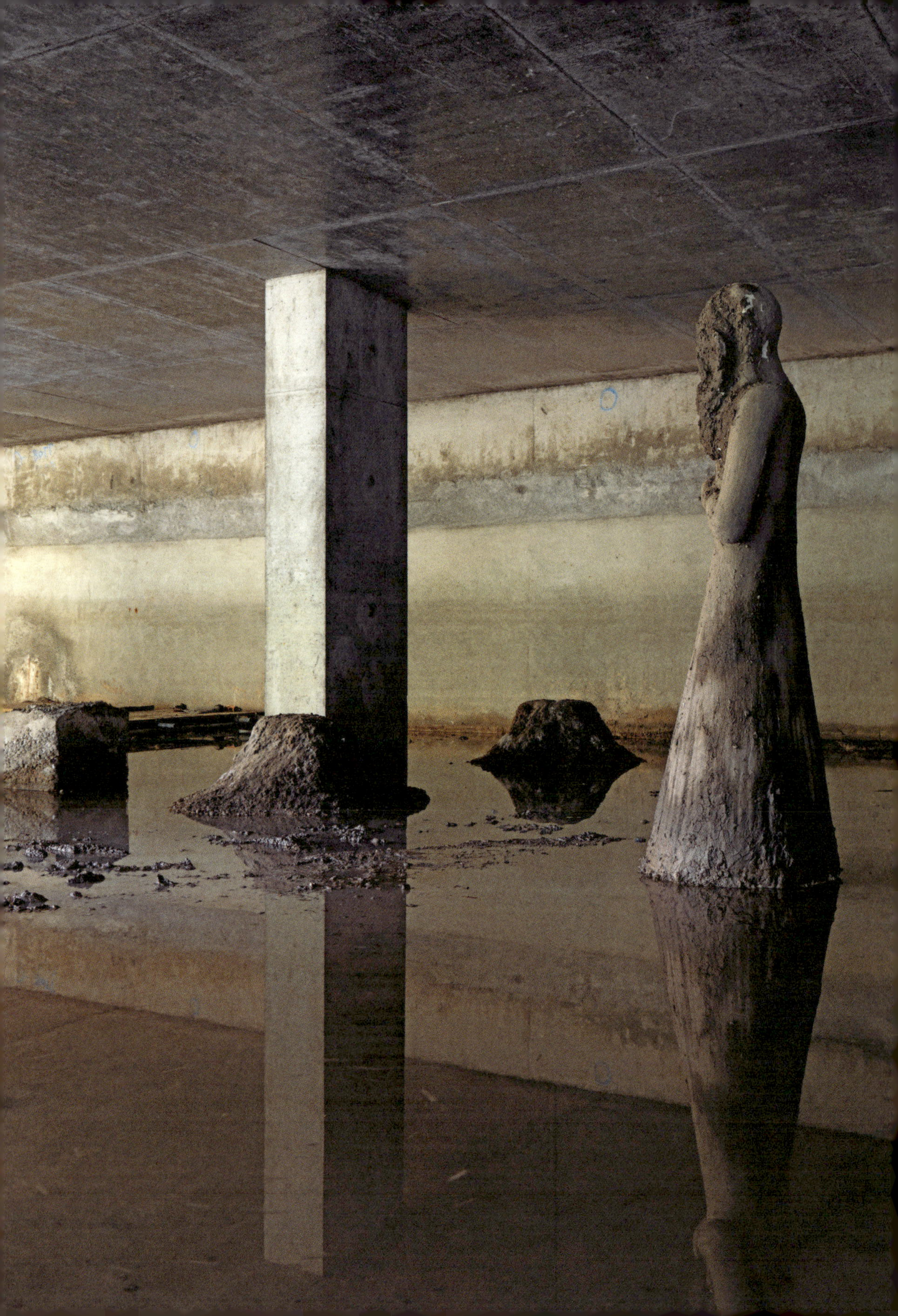

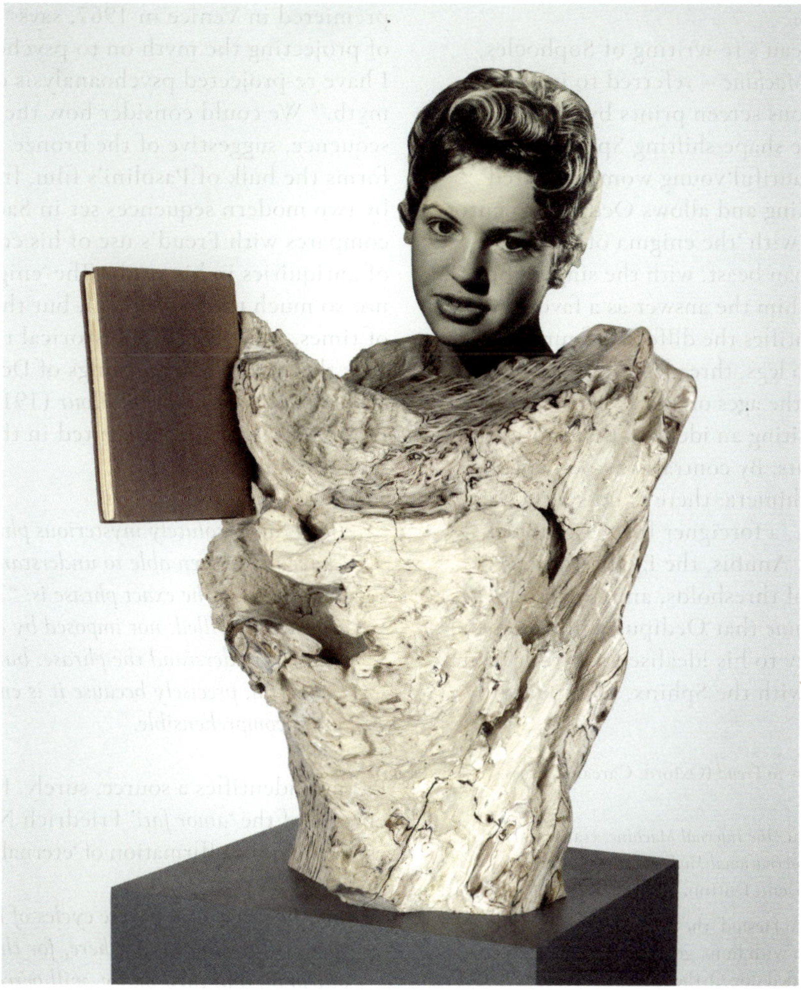

The other day the Professor had reproached me for jerking out my arm and looking at my watch. He had said, "I keep an eye on the time. I will tell you when the session is over. You need not keep looking at the time, as if you were in a hurry to get away"—H.D.[1]

In Jean Cocteau's re-writing of Sophocles, *The Infernal Machine* – referred to in the two eponymous screen prints by Simon Moretti – the shape-shifting Sphinx who appears a beautiful young woman is tired of all the killing and allows Oedipus to enter into contact with 'the enigma of enigmas, with the human beast, with the singing bitch', having given him the answer as a favour.[2] Oedipus identifies the different figures – four legs, two legs, three legs – as belonging to the same, the ages of 'man'. He solves the riddle by positing an identity that unites the three moments. By contrast the body of the Sphinx is a chimera: there is no synthesis.[3] If the Sphinx, a foreigner from Aethopea, is a monster, Anubis, the Egyptian dog-headed god of thresholds, announces in *The Infernal Machine* that Oedipus will become one. Contrary to his idealised self-reflection face to face with the Sphinx, Oedipus will also turn out to be a monster, the plague-causing polluter who must blind and expel himself from the city.[4] However, rather than mirroring her, his monstrousness will be of a different kind.[5]

Pasolini, speaking of his film *Edipo Re* that premiered in Venice in 1967, says 'instead of projecting the myth on to psychoanalysis, I have re-projected psychoanalysis on to the myth.'[6] We could consider how the mythic sequence, suggestive of the bronze age, which forms the bulk of Pasolini's film, framed by two modern sequences set in Sacile, compares with Freud's use of his collection of antiquities in his study. The 'enigma' is not so much the myth itself, but the relation of times, of mythic and historical time – as is the case in the paintings of De Chirico such as *The Enigma of the Hour* (1911). In the interview it is represented in the phrase which fascinates Pasolini:

> *This is an absolutely mysterious phrase, which I have never been able to understand; but it is in Sophocles. The exact phrase is: "There, now all is clear, willed, not imposed by destiny." I cannot understand the phrase, but I find it wonderful, precisely because it is enigmatic and incomprehensible.*[7]

Pasolini identifies a source, surely, for the enigma of the '*amor fati*' Friedrich Nietzsche espouses in the affirmation of 'eternal recurrence':

> *And in every one of these cycles of human life there will be one hour where, for the first time one man, and then many, will perceive the*

1 H.D., *Tribute to Freud* (Oxford: Carcanet Press, 1971), p.17.

2 Jean Cocteau, *The Infernal Machine*, trans. Carl Wildman *International Modern Plays*. (London, New York: Dent; Dutton, 1950), p.196.

3 According to Hesiod, the Sphinx is the daughter of Chimaera with lion-, goat- and snake-heads, and the two-headed dog Orthos who was her brother, therefore she is the product of incest: see Almut-Barbara Renger, *Oedipus and the Sphinx: The Threshold Myth From Sophocles Through Freud to Cocteau*, trans. Duncan Smart, John T. Hamilton and David G. Rice (Chicago: University of Chicago Press, 2013), p.34. For the implications for art of the chimeric, see Michael Newman, 'Florian Hecker: Chimerization and Form,' in *Florian Hecker: Chimerizations*, ed. Robin Mackay, Susanne Gaensheimer and Miguel Wandschneider (Porto; Frankfurt am Main: Culturgest; MMK Museum für Moderne Kunst, 2013), pp.59-90.

4 See Renger, *Oedipus and the Sphinx: The Threshold Myth From Sophocles Through Freud to Cocteau*, pp.26–27.

5 Renger, *Oedipus and the Sphinx: The Threshold Myth From Sophocles Through Freud to Cocteau*, p.40.

6 Oswald. Stack and Pier Paolo Pasolini, *Pasolini on Pasolini; Interviews with Oswald Stack*. (London: Thames and Hudson and BFI, 1969), p.120.

7 Stack and Pasolini, *Pasolini on Pasolini*, p.125.

mighty thought of the eternal recurrence of all things:– and for mankind this is always the hour of Noon.[8]

Noon is when for a moment the shadow of the negative is suspended.

Freud applied the archaeological metaphor very early in his work:

Thus it came about that in this, the first full-length analysis of a hysteria undertaken by me, I arrived at a procedure which I later developed into a regular method and employed deliberately. This procedure was one of clearing away the pathogenic psychical material layer by layer, and we liked to compare it with the technique of excavating a buried city.[9]

Freud's metaphor of archaeology for psycho-analysis suggests an organisation of horizontal layers which one could penetrate going ever deeper.[10] What of the tilting, folding and faulting of strata, and penetration by volcanos and earthquakes? The most ancient comes to the surface, and the recent is buried. A different kind of topology of relations is required, one proposed by Anubis who in *The Infernal Machine* holds up the Sphinx's dress and says:

Look at the folds in this cloth. Crush them together. Now if you pierce this bundle with a pin, remove the pin, smooth the cloth till all trace of the old creases disappears, do you think a simple country loon would believe that the innumerable holes recurring at intervals result from a single thrust of a pin?[11]

Might Linder's careful, patient use of the scalpel to cut out images be compared with the work of the archaeologist, and interpreted as a response to Freud's archaeological metaphor exercised on the body of the female hysteric? The photographic figure is extracted from its context and placed into another, where the viewer is invited to reverie, dream, and projection. The photomontage *Inflora* is commemorative, made soon after the death of the artist's father, and a shell merges with a 1930s hairstyle at the back of the head, the involution alluding to the sculpture of Barbara Hepworth, so in a sense the work contains a relation to both the paternal and the maternal (the latter Freud's blind spot) in a time of anachronism. Photomontage combines different times in the present of the viewing. The title of Linder's mural at Southwark Station, *Bower of Bliss* (2018–19) recalls the description in Edward Spencer's *The Fairie Queene* where Sir Guyon captures the witch Acrasia in a net and destroys her bower, an act of repression of the feminine which is also a story of colonisation, in Ireland and the Americas.[12] At the same time, it is the result of an investigation into the strata of the station, its archaeological layers. The aim, however, is not to bring the concealed to light, but to bring night into day. Jean Cocteau says in an interview:

It is from our reserve, from our night, that things come to us. Our work pre-exists within us. The problem consists in discovering it (invenire). *We are but its archaeologists.*[13]

8 'Notes on the Eternal Recurrence' in *The Complete Works of Friedrich Nietzsche: The First Complete and Authorised English Translation*, trans. Oscar Levy (New York: Gordon Press, 1974), p.250.

9 Josef Breuer, and Sigmund Freud, *Studies on Hysteria* (New York: Basic Books, 1957), p.139.

10 There are many discussions of Freud's archaeological metaphor, and his antiquities. See in particular Richard H. Armstrong, *A Compulsion for Antiquity: Freud and the Ancient World* (Ithaca, NY: Cornell University Press, 2005).

11 Cocteau, *The Infernal Machine*, op. cit., 200.

12 For a brilliant discussion of this, see Stephen Greenblatt, *Renaissance Self-Fashioning: From More to Shakespeare* (Chicago: University of Chicago Press, 1980), pp.157–92, who makes the comparison with the role of renunciation of pleasure in Freud's *Civilization and Its Discontents*, p.174.

13 Translated and quoted in Renger, *Oedipus and the Sphinx: The Threshold Myth From Sophocles Through Freud to Cocteau*, 65. from J. Cocteau, Entretiens autour du cinématographe, ed. André Fraigneau (Paris, 1951), p.159.

fig.19

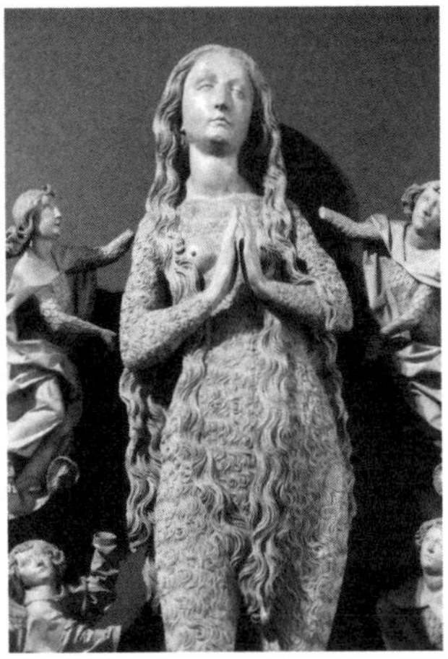

The carved, limewood figure of Paloma Varga Weisz's sculpture *Lazlo's dream* has six breasts and floppy dog's ears. We cannot know the sex exactly, or whether this is a human or an animal. As well as the German limewood sculptures of the Renaissance, we might think of Tilman Riemenschneider's limewood *Mary Magdalene surrounded by angels* (1490-95, Munich) in which Mary is covered in body hair, echoed in Varga Weisz's *Haarige Frau* (Hairy Woman) (1999-2000) where the figure seems to be emerging from the more raw-cut wood some of which is left over her head as well as forming the base,[14] although the smallness of both of Varga Weisz's sculptures suggests a remoteness, or the miniaturisation of the dream.[15] The combination of human with animal features in *Lazlo's dream* also recalls one of the earliest of human carvings, the 40,000 year old Ice Age lion man carved in mammoth ivory, with the body of a human and the head of a lion. Does not the figure of *Lazlo's dream* seem like a relative of the terracotta figurine of the Sphinx from the 5th to 4th century BC in Freud's collection, between male and female, human head and lioness's body, earth bound and with wings? The monstrous of the mixing of categories is not the same exactly as the monstrousness of Oedipus's 'eye too many',[16] and transgression of the limits of the paternal law.

Man, bent (2019) – a hint of perversion in the title – is Varga Weisz's sculpture in Freud's study across from the couch on the other side of the table of antiquities, a life-size limewood young man jointed like an artist's figurine is offering his ass for a beating. This cannot but evoke Freud's paper 'A child is being beaten', which was an important advance in the understanding of masochism, as well as the modality of fantasy, through the relation to Oedipal desire.[17] It is largely directed at the beating phantasies of women, drawn, it must be said, from Freud's analysis of his daughter Anna. The fantasy has three stages: 'My father is beating the child whom I hate'; 'I am beaten by my father'; others, mostly boys, are being beaten by an authority figure who is not the father but a representative. In *Man, bent* the viewer becomes the observer of a reconstruction of a *tableau vivant* – the mode used by both Hans Bellmer in his photos of the doll, and Pierre Klossowski in his novels, drawings and sculptures. Given that the figure is life-size, there is something like an uncanny shock. Acting out in a space of words.

The group of sculptures by Daniel Silver from which *Moon Face* (2018) comes were modelled fast in clay in response to dancers that were invited to the studio. While they were made and displayed on tables with Freud's antiquities in mind, they also draw

14 Thanks to Simon Moretti for drawing my attention to *Haarige Frau*. For an illustration, see Mariana Vecellio, ed., *Paloma Varga Weisz: Root of a Dream*, exh. cat. Castello di Rivoli Museo d'Arte Contemporanea (Milan: Mousse Publishing, 2017), pp.78-79.

15 See Michael. Baxandall, *The Limewood Sculptors of Renaissance Germany* (New Haven: Yale University Press, 1980), who writes, drawing on Paracelsus, of the 'chairomancy' of the limewood sculptors, p.32.

16 The phrase 'Perhaps King Oedipus had an eye too many', suggesting the excess of his interpretation and pursuit of knowledge, is from Hölderlin's late poem 'In Lovely Blue'. Friedrich Hölderlin, '*In lieblicher Bläue*' [In Lovely Blue], *Hymns and Fragments*, trans. Richard Sieburth (Princeton: Princeton University Press, 1984), pp.247-53.

17 Sigmund Freud, '"A Child is Being Beaten". A Contribution to the Study of the Origin of Sexual Perversions,' in *The Standard Edition of the Complete Psychological Works of Sigmund Freud, Volume XVII (1917-1919): An Infantile Neurosis and Other Works* (1955).

on Auguste Rodin's procedure of drawing and modelling in the presence of a dancer. Rodin's achievement was to transform figure sculpture from being the representation of the body to being the embodiment in a plastic object of the temporal existence of the human being. This project was taken up by Giacometti, who created some very small sculptures that feel as if they are simultaneously present and receding out of the grasp. Sometimes they recall Greek *kouroi* or hieratic Egyptian sculpture. Existence in the present takes on an archaic dimension.

Rilke in the poem 'Archaic Torso of Apollo' distinguishes between the head which is 'mysterious' and the torso from which 'gleaming light is shed'.[18] This is reminiscent of Daniel Silver putting separate heads of stone on mannequin bodies, or heads of bronze on Pietrasanta marble. There is a reference to Roman busts in these heads of marble and yellow onyx. The element of direct carving could be related to *damnatio memoriae*, the 'condemnation of memory', when a statue was defaced. The object of memory becomes a site of effacement. The fleeting gesture may be seen as both a 'pathos formula' in Aby Warburg's sense, like the words or tropes of a language of gesture carried through history.[19] At the same time they suggest the capture in the slow time of stone of a fleeting moment of the body that, as the Exhibition Guide suggests, is reminiscent of the casts at Pompeii of bodies asphyxiated and buried by lava. This was a very important source of archaeological metaphor for Freud, and Pompeii is the location of Jensen's novel *Gradiva* which he analysed. The fleeting moment of the movement or gesture of the head in Silver's sculpture could be compared with the relief of the fleeting gait of the woman's leg which Hannold fetishizes.[20]

Pompeii has also stood for the 'end' not just of a Roman town in 79AD, but also of 'civilization' and even of the human species – a role that it adopted after Hiroshima and Nagasaki, the dropping of nuclear bombs that Alix Strachey refers to in *The Unconscious Motives of War* (1957):

> *already by now the use of only a few hydrogen bombs in a war between the major Powers would put an end, if not to mankind altogether, at any rate to human civilisation; and a couple of thousand of them will destroy not only mankind but every form of life on earth.*[21]

For *Co-operation* (2019) Goshka Macuga has made jug-portraits of Alix Strachey and Joan Rivière, best known as the author of 'Womanliness as Masquerade', the first analysis of the feminine as performative,[22] to join that of Freud. The jug is also, as Heidegger – of whom Macuga has shown a vase elsewhere – reminds us, modelled around a void.[23] In opening up the bust by making it a vase or jug, Macuga also questions traditional notions of interiority and exteriority, with the surface as physiognomic expression, as, indeed, did psychoanalysis. Macuga often shows these vases with flowers or fronds. Ceramic head vases became popular in the 1950s, when they often depicted female movie stars. They could

fig.20

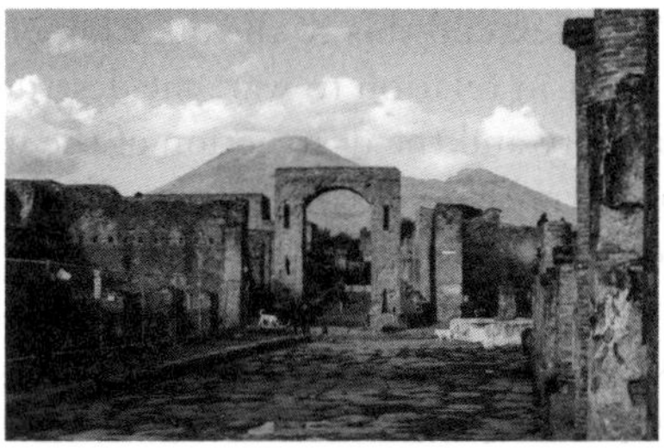

18 See Rainer Maria Rilke, Jessie Lemont, and Hans Trausil, *Rodin* (London: The Grey Walls Press Ltd, 1946).

19 See Colleen Becker, 'Aby Warburg's Pathosformel as Methodological Paradigm,' *Journal of Art Historiography*, 9 (2013).

20 Sigmund Freud, 'Delusions and Dreams in Jensen's Gradiva,' in *The Standard Edition of the Complete Psychological Works of Sigmund Freud, Volume IX (1906-1908): Jensen's 'Gradiva'and Other Works* (1959).

21 Alix Strachey, *The Unconscious Motives of War: A Psycho-Analytical Contribution* (London: George Allan & Unwin, 1957), p.8.

22 Its first publication was in *The Internaional Journal of Psychoanalysis*, Vol.10 (1929), pp.35-44.

23 For the discussion of the jug, see Martin Heidegger, 'The Thing' in *Poetry, Language, Thought*, trans. Albert Hofstadter (New York: Harper & Row, 1975), pp.165-82.

also be compared with 'toby jugs', supposedly modelled on Sir Toby Belch from Shakespeare's *Twelfth Night*. So they are both decorative and celebratory, undermining the authority of the traditional portrait-bust, while conversely in the case of the women analysts, honouring those women psychoanalysts, translators and supporters of Freud who are not normally attributed sufficient authority.

A question raised by Alix Strachey's book is both what contribution psychoanalysis may make to understanding human aggression and destructiveness and also how the prospect of the outcome of that history combined with science in the nuclear bomb, leading to the potential destruction of mankind, affects psychoanalysis itself. And what does it mean that this is put forward by a woman? Macuga, too, explored the idea of the end of the human, and the post-human, in *To the Son of Man who Ate the Scroll* at the Prada Foundation in 2016. The inspiration for the part of that exhibition comprising a network of linked bronze heads of thinkers came from the exchange of letters between Freud and Einstein on the future of humankind, collected in the book *Why War?*, published in 1933 by The International Institute for Intellectual Co-operation of the League of Nations, which recalls the title of the work at the Freud Museum. There was once a utopian dimension to the standpoint on the end which seems to be absent today.

If Goshka Macuga makes a dummy of 'Cesare' from *The Cabinet of Dr Caligari*, this is to replicate what takes place in the film, where there is already a dummy meant to deceive pursuers/detectives while the somnambulist is performing his murders. There is much that could be said of the relation of psychoanalysis to somnambulism, with its implications of suggestibility and automatism, and its importance to the psychology of Janet which Freud investigated as a prelude to his own analytical breakthroughs in the treatment of hysteria. The reference to *Dr Caligari* taking control of the somnambulist and making him commit murder raises the question of the political subject of fascism induced to perform unethical deeds under the control of a hypnotic master.

In the installation of the exhibition at the Freud Museum, the dummy somnambulist situated on the floor of The Anna Freud Room echoes Varga Weisz's *Man, bent* before the couch in Freud's study, reminding us once again of Freud's analysis of Anna that gave rise to both 'A child is being beaten' and her very first paper as an analyst, 'Beating Fantasies and Daydreams' (1922).

fig.21

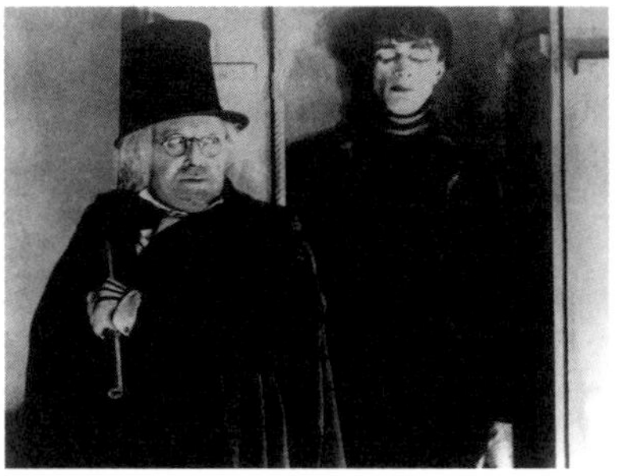

The film *The Cabinet of Dr Caligari* directed by Robert Weine employs a *mise-en-abîme*: the protagonist/investigator ends up as a patient in the asylum directed by the character that he is investigating. Richard Armstrong discerns this structure in the way Freud interprets the play *Oedipus the King* in terms of its effect through *Hamlet*.[24] The relation of the court to the play within the play, the 'Mousetrap', is the relation of the audience to *Oedipus*, confronting their own repressed wish, and explains its effect. The *mise-en-abîme* produces a structure of implication whereby the audience is folded in to what they are watching.

We can extend this to the question of standpoint in relation to war, the destruction of humanity and the destruction of the planet. The problem is to create a standpoint that is both one of knowledge (which is necessarily distanced, and in the Western tradition, scopic), and *at the same time* one of implication. The very standpoint – absolutely necessary as it is – is a part of the structure that produced the disaster.

24 Richard H Armstrong, 'The Tragedy of Hoemdiplet: Freud's Fusion of Oedipus and Hamlet,' *Codex: Revista de Estudos Clássicos*, 6, no.2 (2018).

The idea of the end is also implied in Simon Moretti's neon text work *Only Day and Night* (2019). The end here is from the Epilogue of Herman Melville's novel *Moby Dick*, for Moretti's words could be a parapractic misreading of 'for almost one whole day and night', which is when Ishmael, having been sucked down to the centre of the vortex of the sinking whaler Pequod is thrown up with a coffin-like buoy, is floating on the water circled by 'unharming sharks'. If another work by Moretti in the show, made in collaboration with his collaborator Goshka Macuga, the screen print *Encounters in the Field* (2019), concerns the transmission of ideas that takes place through *The International Journal of Psychoanalysis* and in other ways, *Only Day and Night* reminds us that the anachronistic temporality of 'the enigma of the hour' raises, once again, a question of survival.

fig.19 Tilman Riemenschneider, *Heilige Magdalena von Engeln erhoben*, 1490/92.
fig.20 Pompeii archaeological site, Pompeii Italy.
fig.21 Werner Krauss and Conrad Veidt, *The Cabinet of Dr. Caligari*, 1920, directed by Robert Wiene.
fig.22 Goshka Macuga & Simon Moretti, *Encounters in the Field*, 2019.

fig.22

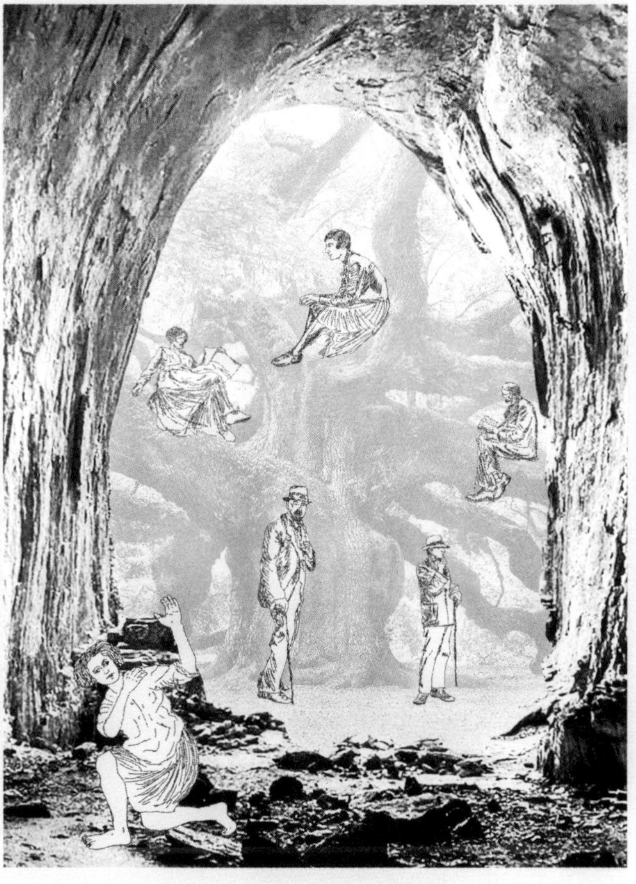

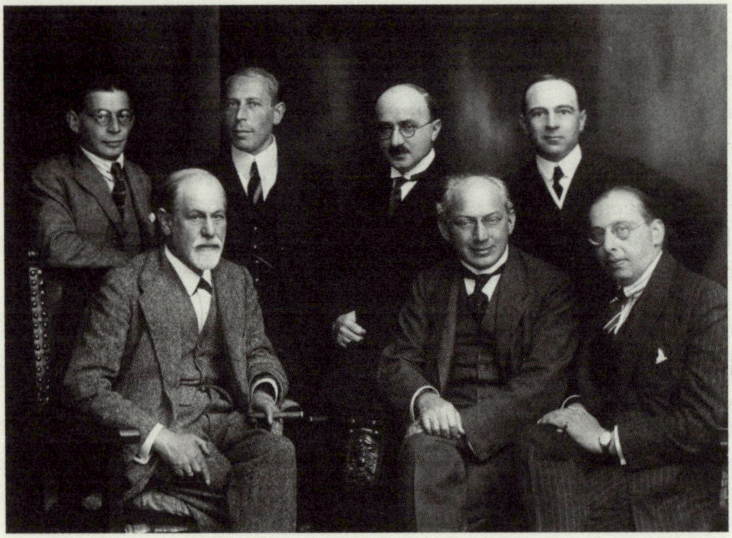

1

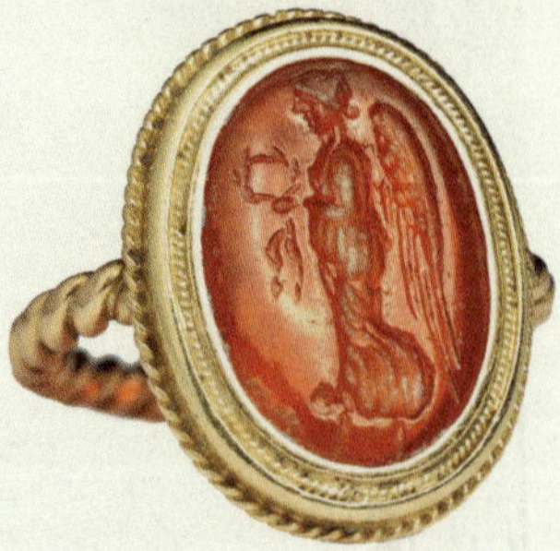

2

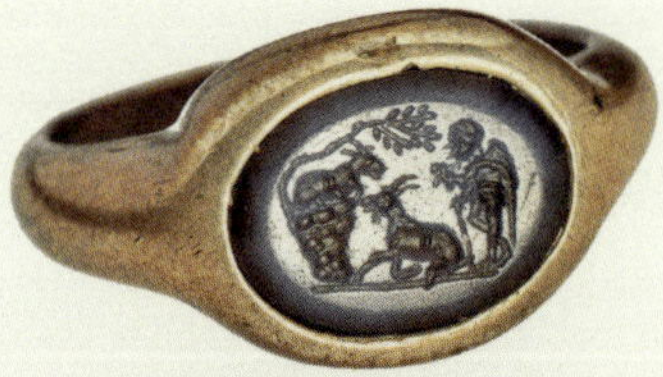

3

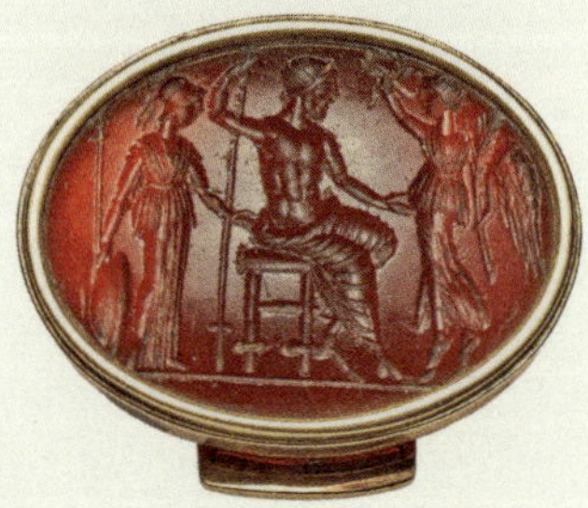

4

1 Photograph of Freud's Secret Committee, 1922 Sigmund Freud, Sándor Ferenczi, Hanns Sachs, Otto Rank, Karl Abraham. Museum no. IN0145. Collection of the Freud Museum London

2 *Gold Ring with Intaglio depicting Victory.* Ring of Twisted gold, with fixed mounted carnelian intaglio depicting Victory holding a laurel leaf. Belonged to Anna Freud. Museum no. 6427. Collection of the Freud Museum London.

3 *Silver Ring with Blue Glass Intaglio*, Roman, 1st Century AD (setting 20th century). Silver ring with blue intaglio of a pastoral scene of a goat-herd with two goats, given by Freud to Ernst Simmel in 1928. Stamped inside 'EP' & '800'. Museum no. 5046. Collection of the Freud Museum London.

4 *Roman Intaglio depicting Jupiter, Victory and Minerva.* Roman carnelian intaglio depicting Jupiter enthroned, crowned by Victory, with Minerva in attendance. Originally set in Sigmund Freud's ring. Set in a modern clip belonging to Anna Freud. Museum no. 2016.7. Collection of the Freud Museum London.

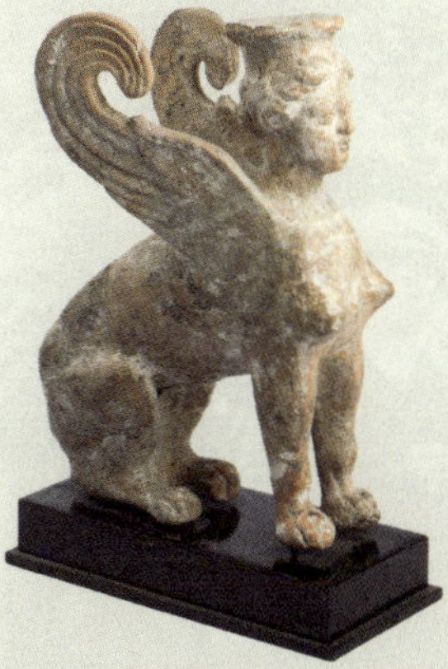

5

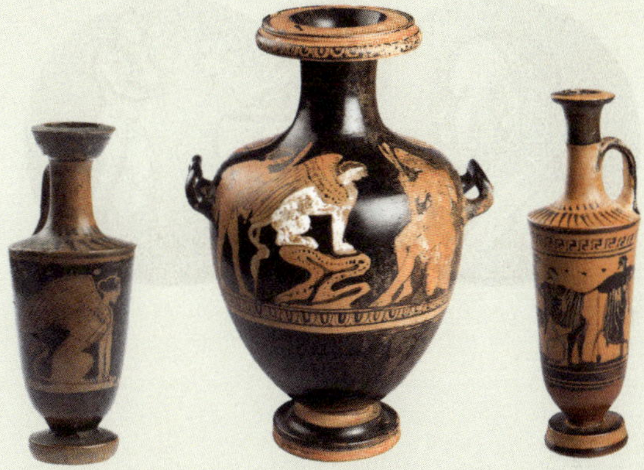

6,7,8

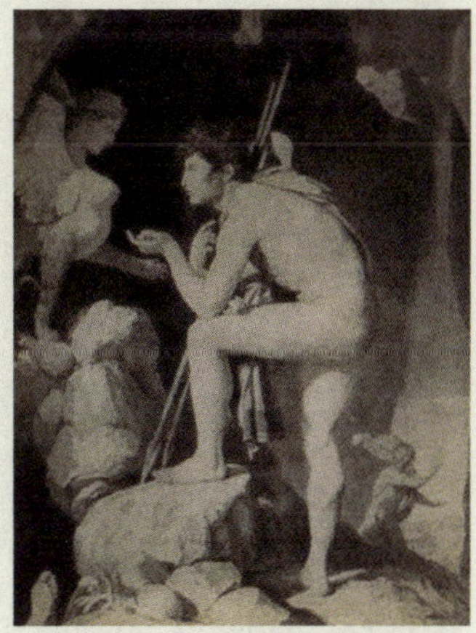

10

9

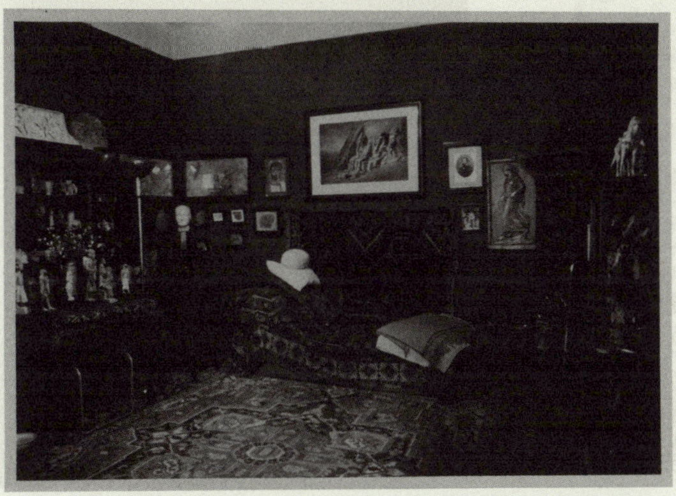

5 *Figure of Sphinx*, Southern Italian, late 5th to early 4th century BC. Museum no. 4387. Collection of the Freud Museum London

6 *Red-figure lekythos decorated with sphinx*, 3 Classical Period late 5th century BC. Museum no. 4466. Collection of the Freud Museum London

7 *Red-figure hydria showing Oedipus and the Sphinx*, Greek, 380–360BC. Museum no. 3117. Collection of the Freud Museum London

8 *Black-figure lekythos decorated with Sphinx and the Elders*, late 5th century BC. Museum no. 3683. Collection of the Freud Museum London

9 Photograph of Berggasse 19 interior, Vienna, by Edmund Engelman, 1938. Museum number IN1270. Collection of the Freud Museum London

10 Reproduction engraving of *Oedipus and the Sphinx* by Ingres belonging to Freud, 25.2 × 20.6 × 2.3 cm. Museum no. 6405. Collection of the Freud Museum London

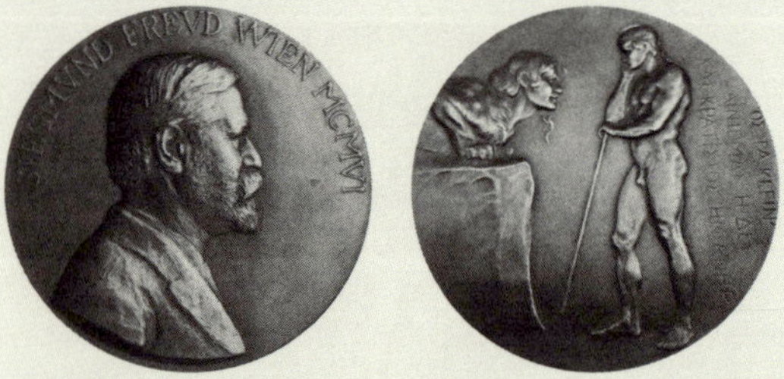

11

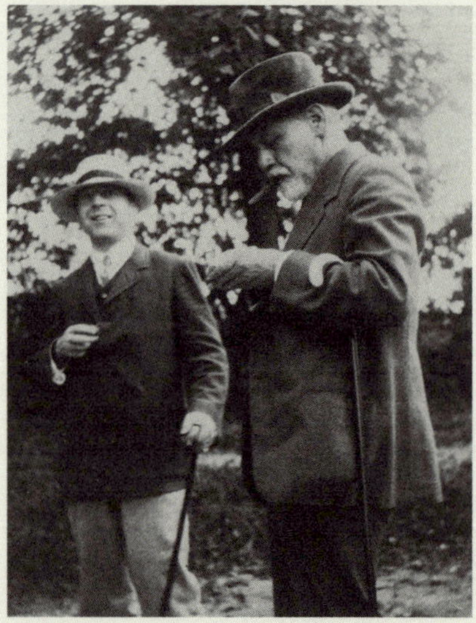

13

12

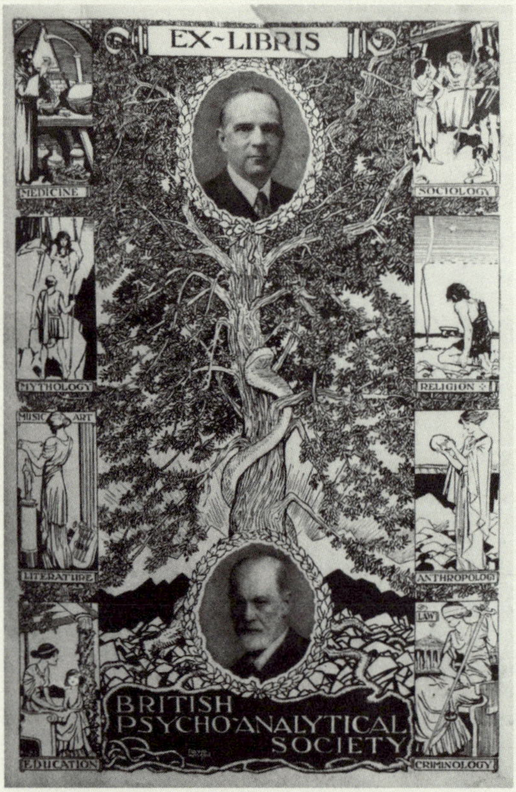

14

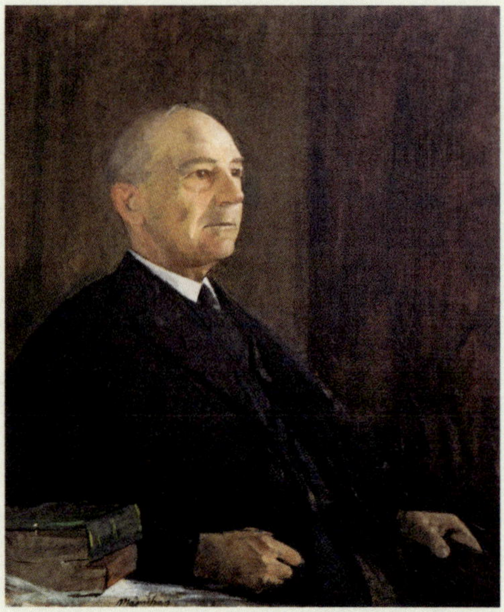

11 Medal commemorating Freud's 50th birthday, 1906, bronze, designed by C. M. Schwerdtner. Museum no. 4395. Collection of the Freud Museum London

12 Bookplate of the British Psychoanalytical Society with Freud and Ernest Jones, date unknown, designed by David Wilson. Collection of the British Psychoanalytical Society

13 Photograph of Freud and Ernest Jones, 1920. Museum no. IN0137. Collection of the Freud Museum London

14 Rodrigo Moynihan, *Ernest Jones*, 1946 Oil on canvas, 97.4 × 84.7 cm. Collection of the British Psychoanalytical Society

15

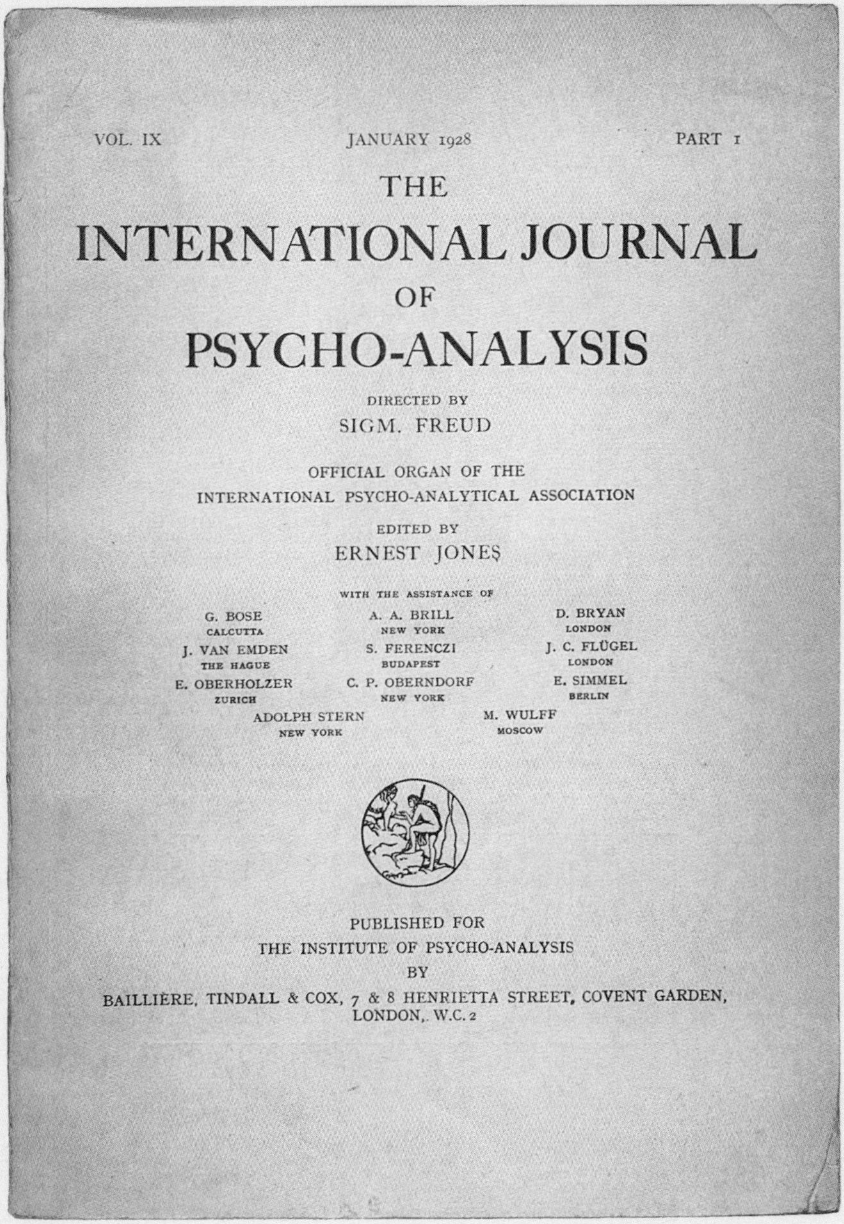

VOL. IX — JANUARY 1928 — PART 1

THE
INTERNATIONAL JOURNAL
OF
PSYCHO-ANALYSIS

DIRECTED BY
SIGM. FREUD

OFFICIAL ORGAN OF THE
INTERNATIONAL PSYCHO-ANALYTICAL ASSOCIATION

EDITED BY
ERNEST JONES

WITH THE ASSISTANCE OF

G. BOSE, CALCUTTA — A. A. BRILL, NEW YORK — D. BRYAN, LONDON
J. VAN EMDEN, THE HAGUE — S. FERENCZI, BUDAPEST — J. C. FLÜGEL, LONDON
E. OBERHOLZER, ZURICH — C. P. OBERNDORF, NEW YORK — E. SIMMEL, BERLIN
ADOLPH STERN, NEW YORK — M. WULFF, MOSCOW

PUBLISHED FOR
THE INSTITUTE OF PSYCHO-ANALYSIS
BY
BAILLIÈRE, TINDALL & COX, 7 & 8 HENRIETTA STREET, COVENT GARDEN,
LONDON, W.C. 2

15 *The International Journal of Psychoanalysis* vol IX PART 1, 1928. Collection of the Freud Museum London

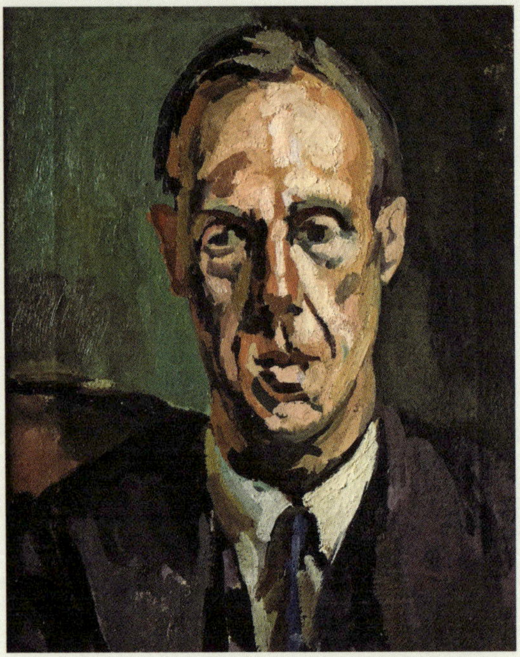

16

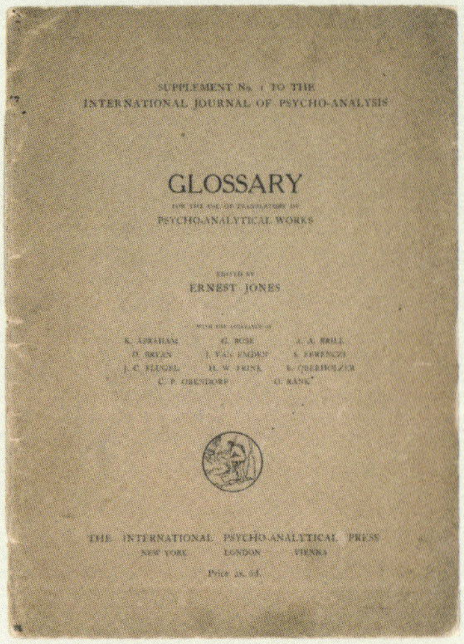

19

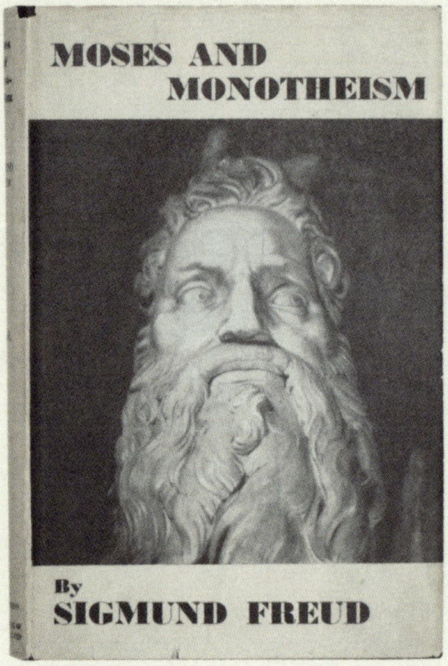

17

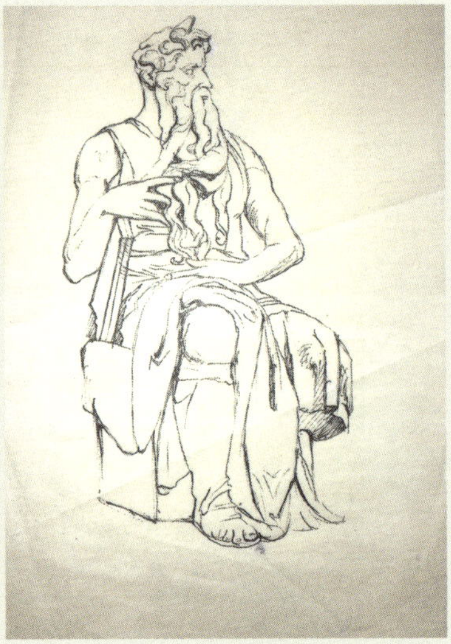

18

16 *Adrian Stephen* (third editor and brother of Virginia Woolf) by Duncan Grant, c.late 1930s–mid 1940s. Oil on canvas, 57 × 49 cm. Collection of the British Psychoanalytical Society

17 *Moses and Monotheism*, Sigmund Freud, Hogarth Press and The Institute of Psycho-Analysis, London, 1939. Collection of the Freud Museum London

18 Drawing of Michelangelo's Moses (drawn or commissioned by Freud), 1912. Ink on paper. Museum no. 6417. Collection of the Freud Museum London

19 *Glossary for the Use of Translators of Psycho-Analytical Works*, edited by Ernest Jones, 1924. Published as a supplement to *The International Journal of Psycho-Analysis* for The Institute of Psycho-Analysis by Baillère, Tindall and Cox. Collection of the British Psychoanalytical Society

20

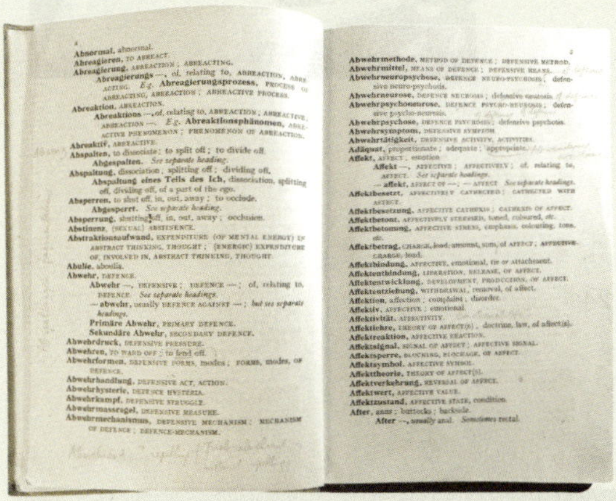

21

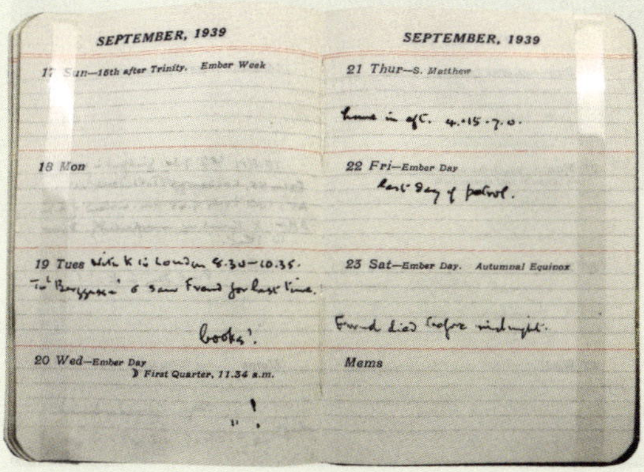

SEPTEMBER, 1939

17 Sun—16th after Trinity. Ember Week

18 Mon

19 Tues

20 Wed—Ember Day
First Quarter, 11.34 a.m.

SEPTEMBER, 1939

21 Thur—S. Matthew

22 Fri—Ember Day

23 Sat—Ember Day. Autumnal Equinox

Mems

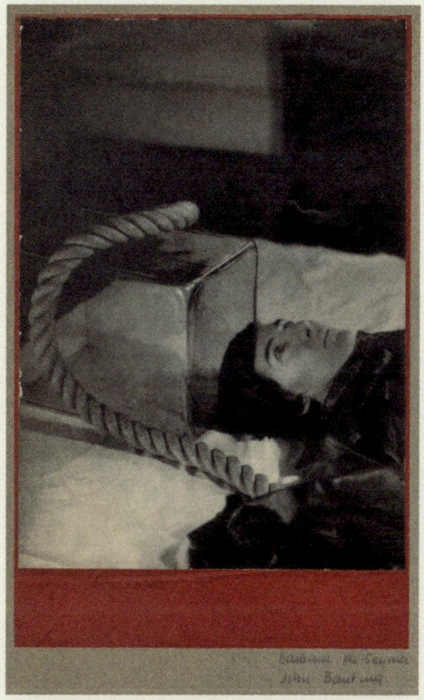

22

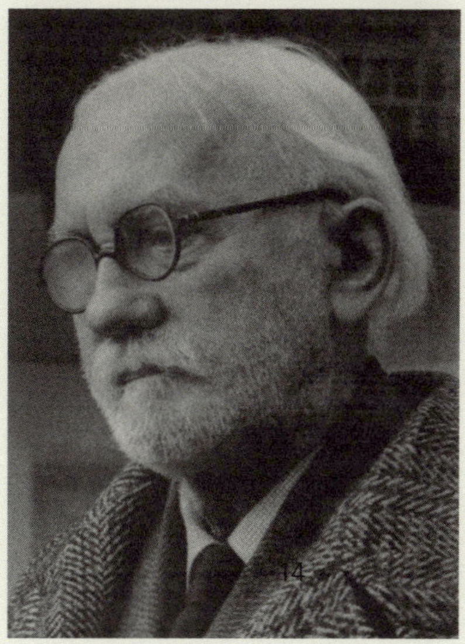

23

20 *A New German-English Psycho-analytical Vocabulary* by Alix Strachey, 1943
Published as a supplement to *The International Journal of Psycho-Analysis* for The Institute of Psycho-Analysis by Baillère, Tindall and Cox. Collection of the British Psychoanalytical Society

21 Ernest Jones's diary, 1939. Entries September 19 Tue 'To "Berggasse" I saw Freud for the last time', September 22 Fri 'last day of petrol', September 23 Sat 'Freud died before midnight'. Collection of the British Psychoanalytical Society

22 Barbara Ker-Seymer and John Banting, *Alix Strachey*, 1930. Bromide print on red card mount, 30 × 21 cm. National Portrait Gallery, ref. n.13131

23 Photo of James Strachey in his older years, 1960s. After a series of eye operations he wore glasses with one opaque lens. Collection of the British Psychoanalytical Society

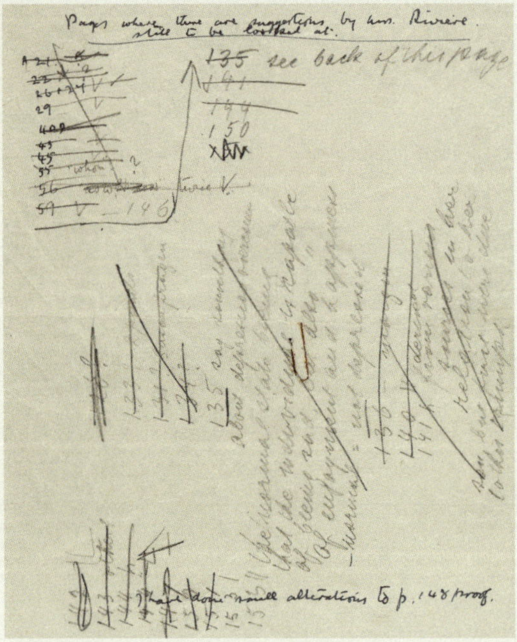

24

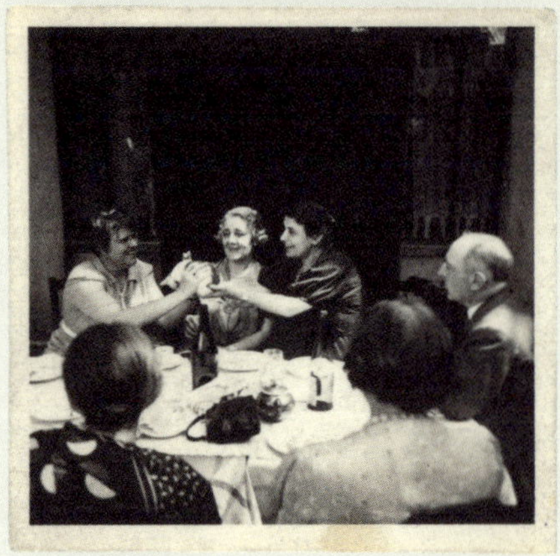

25

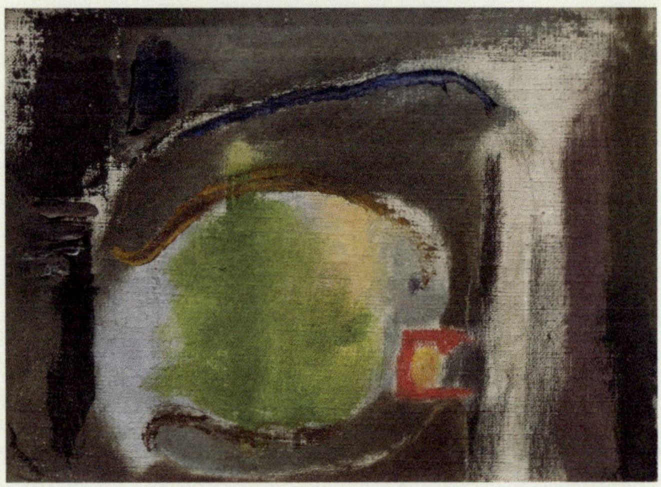

26

24 Melanie Klein notes. Courtesy Wellcome Collection, London and Melanie Klein Archive
25 Photograph of Melanie Klein, Anna Freud and Ernest Jones. Courtesy Wellcome Collection, London and Melanie Klein Archive
26 *A Thought Too Big for its Concept* by psychoanalyst, author and artist Marion Milner, 1990. Oil on canvas, 38 × 48 cm. Collection of the British Psychoanalytical Society

27, 28

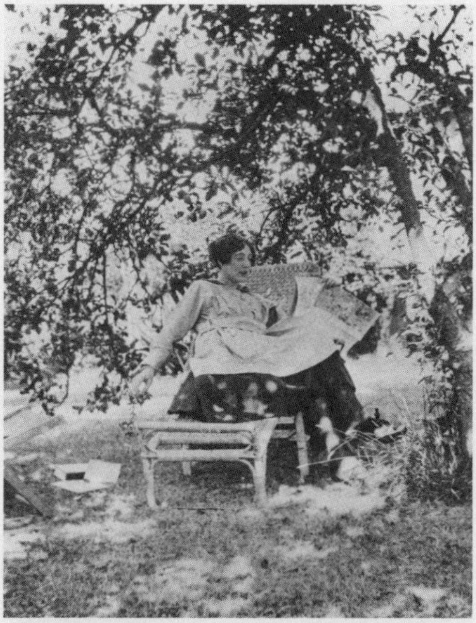

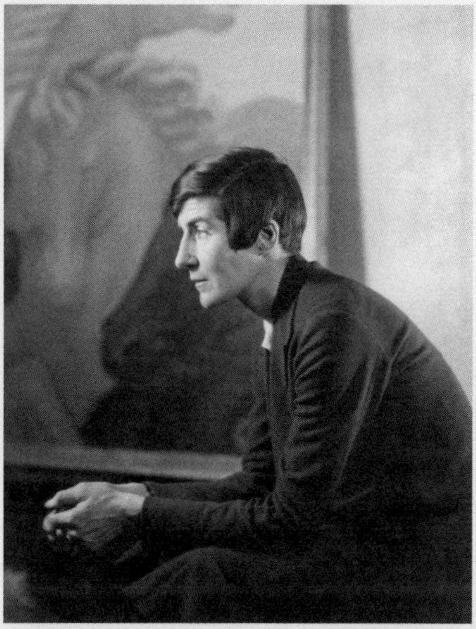

29, 30

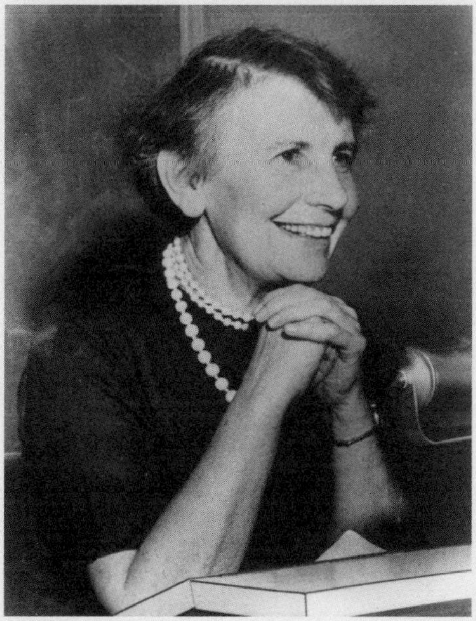

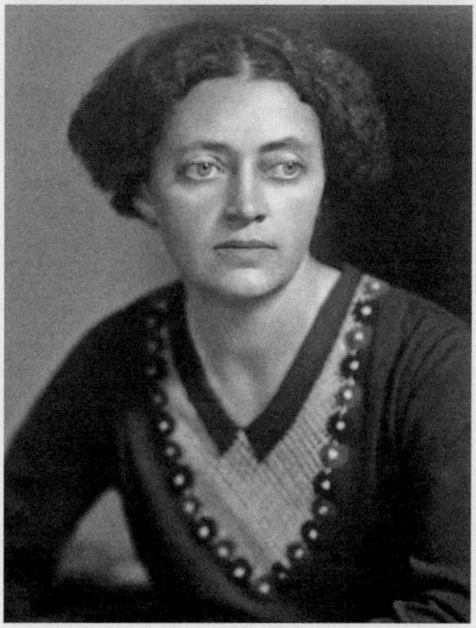

27 Photograph of Joan Riviere psychoanalyst and translation editor for *The International Journal of Psychoanalysis*, c.1912/13. Collection of the British Psychoanalytical Society

28 Photograph of Alix Strachey psychoanalyst and translator by Barbara Ker-Seymer bromide print on green tissue and card mount, 1930s. National Portrait Gallery, ref. n.13132

29 Photograph of Anna Freud psychoanalyst and translator, date unknown. Collection of the British Psychoanalytical Society

30 Photograph of Marjorie Brierley psychoanalyst, c.1920, who made a significant contribution to *The International Journal of Psychoanalysis*. Collection of the British Psychoanalytical Society

JH Thank you so much. And thank you very much for the invitation to Simon and the other curators.

I found it really fascinating wandering around this house, which is so full of riches from the past and the present moment. It's a great reminder that every object ever made was once contemporary and so every object in a sense can have a conversation across time. So, I thought I would start actually, with a little quote from the curators, Simon Moretti, Goshka Macuga and Dana Birksted-Breen, about this exhibition:

fig.23

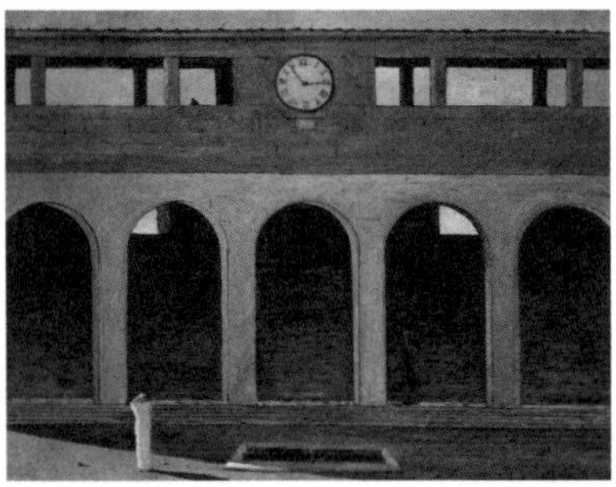

The Enigma of the Hour, the title of the exhibition, takes its inspiration from a painting by Giorgio de Chirico. De Chirico, a contemporary of Freud, evokes with his paintings some of the disturbing states of mind that we encounter in the 'analytic hour' of the consulting room, those states in which devastation and ensuing emptiness and anomy take over, empty of others, distorted, timeless. The enigma in the analytic hour, an 'hour' both timeless and strictly bound by time, the search for an answer, which can never be fully found.

Simon, what was the evolution of the show?

SM Dana Birksted-Breen the Editor-in-chief of *The International Journal of Psychoanalysis* had the initial idea of doing an exhibition here at the Freud Museum for the centenary of the journal and to have contemporary art in conversation with the archive of the *Journal*. She invited Goshka who then invited me. Dana suggested some of the initial themes and then together as a curatorial team, we moved forward and invited the other artists to be guests in our project. Goshka and I also made new work inspired by our research into the archive of the journal. Dana put together a group of psychoanalysts and researchers from all over the world that we called the Exhibition Group who became an incredible source of information and asset to the research. They were instrumental in inspiring us in terms of some of the ideas and how to develop the themes we started off with and in pointing out some of the interesting personalities from the journal's past that you will see in the more historical presentation in the display case upstairs.

We appropriated the title from a painting by Giorgio de Chirico, a contemporary of Freud, who was also very interested in subjects like the unconscious and dreams. De Chirico said that he was never directly influenced by Freud and that he wasn't aware of Freud's writing until at least 1920. The painting *The Enigma of the Hour* is an early metaphysical painting from 1911 and is very much about de Chirico's philosophical interest in time, metaphysical time and Nietzsche's concept of the *Eternal Return*.

JH Daniel, as an artist, in this show, what's the role of Freud in your work?

DS I first came to visit the Freud Museum when I was going to analysis not far away from here. I came here to examine this space and as a sculptor I was really drawn to the collection of Greek and Roman sculptures, which Freud was collecting in 1910 in Vienna. It was the kind of thing that a lot of people were doing and was quite fashionable at the time. Freud was choosing these works, which suited his ideas, he was reading a lot about Greek mythology, and so he could write and have a Greek sculpture in front of him. In his room I could examine his ideas not only as an analyst, but as a curator and as an obsessive collector. That was something that I was very interested in, understanding him in a kind of sculptural way.

JH How is that manifested in your sculptures?

DS I was very lucky, this is 12 years ago, I came here with a digital camera and took photographs (pp.52, 65, 91) of a lot of works which interested me. I walked around in the study. There are very, very small heads, and each one's got a base, which Freud himself had made especially. He would go to the museum in Vienna and order bases to be made especially for his collection by the technician in the museum.

I took photographs of all of these and I walked around with these photographs for about two years not knowing how the images will come into my work then I started a discussion with Artangel who produce projects with artists outside of galleries. I started modelling these images in clay, but not really knowing where it was going to go and that was the beginning of five years discussion with Artangel about a project, which then ended up as *DIG* (p.66). Which was about the analyst, the sculptor and the archaeologist. So digging in three senses of the word, which follows through in the work.

fig.24

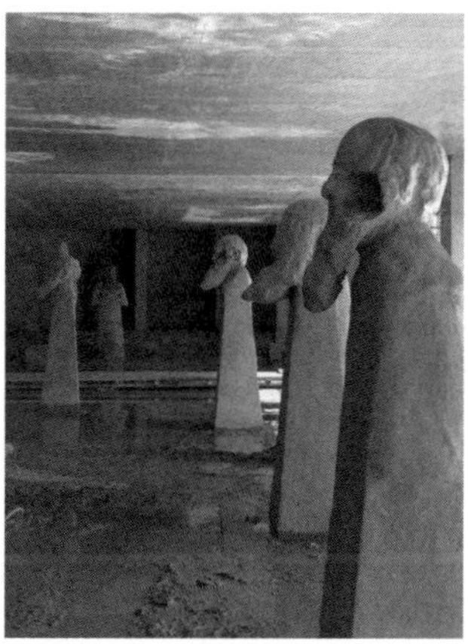

JH You placed those sculptures on the site of an old cinema – and of course, cinema was invented at the same time as psychoanalysis. It's a really nice connection, in terms of the flickering lights in the unconscious or in the theatre.

DS And you'd walk into the building site, which had been a carpark, there aren't many sites in the centre of London we could use. The concrete shell became a place to create this sculptural expedition.

SM It felt like going underground and like an excavation site, the idea of excavation in psychoanalysis.

In the study some of those sculptures come from graves and burial grounds so you're thinking about being underground, a good metaphor for the unconscious. Independently from each other, and from this project, we both had already done a lot of research into Freud, we were both fascinated with his collection.

JH What was your particular interest?

SM I was very much interested in Freud's concept of the Archaeology of the Mind. And this is something I've been exploring for a long time. I had already used images of figures from Freud's collection, and images of Berrgasse 19, as part of some of my collages and photomontages. I was also familiar with some of his writing and I became interested in his concept of Parapraxis as I had started, coincidentally, a new series of neon works which is based on an archive of misreadings of mine.

JH It's like a Freudian slip.

SM This is a new body of work and one neon is currently on display in the study. I seem to misread things regularly and I came up with these kind of metaphysical phrases that lie somewhere between a found text and a new poem, so I started building this alternative archive. This goes hand in hand with the archive of images that I constantly collect in my studio, which are then used in my collages and photomontages. They are both separate activities but in both of them there is an element of free association and the unconscious as a way of making.

JH I was looking at that picture in the back of this room; it's actually *Nine Views of Austria*, but I thought it was called *Nice Views of Austria*.

SM I believe there's only a short passage where Freud actually wrote about parapraxis and about misreadings and mishearings in *The Psychopathology of Everyday Life*. He mentions a funny story that while on holiday, because he was such an obsessive avid collector he would misread shop signs thinking they said 'antiques' when they didn't.

That was a good way of connecting the two, the collection and the misreadings.

JH So, was the work you included in this show made specifically for it?

fig.25

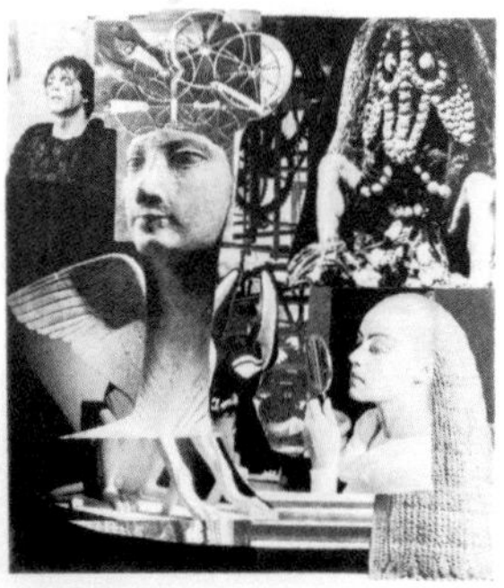

SM Yes, they were very much influenced and chosen with the space in mind and the research as a background. For example my black-and-white screen prints deal with the iconography of the myth and the story of Oedipus in film and theatre. And, of course, this was influenced by the genealogy of the logo of the journal, which is a stylised version of the *Oedipus and the Sphinx* painting by Ingres (p.4), the print of which usually can be found in Freud's study but which is now on display upstairs.

JH Did you choose artists who you knew were interested in Freud, or artists whose work embodies certain ideas of the unconscious?

SM The way I approach choosing artists in my curatorial process is the same as the process of making my work and in fact, I see the curatorial process as just an extension of the making of my work, the two things are interlinked. It's like stepping out of my work and expanding into space. I always start in an instinctive way with free association, I get attracted to things without questioning it at first, it's a very organic process. Connections surface more and more afterwards. The beginning is an automatic process which is the same way I construct an image if I'm making a collage and in fact, I always feel that my shows are kind of collages in themselves.

With someone like Daniel, I realised we already had so much in common, he was also inspired by Freud and there was a connection on this level but then with Linder and Paloma Varga Weisz I thought they would bring a really fresh way of approaching the project. Goshka was very interested in Freud already but from a different point of view, in fact, a large project that she did for the Prada Foundation was partly inspired by a letter from Einstein to Freud, a correspondence on violence, peace and human nature, where they talk about the need for great minds to come together to help humanity forge a better future.

JH And then a sculptor like Paloma Varga Weisz. Her wooden figure on the floor of Freud's study in a sense embodies ideas around the uncanny; it looks so dislocated and out of time and space.

SM The works selected really made sense to me in the context of psychoanalysis and of Freud's theories. Another reference was the Oedipus myth, the idea of enigmas and things that are somehow sphinxes in themselves and the classical references that Freud was of course very interested in. I also found a common interest in the classical with Linder too, and I believe it's something she has been exploring recently.

fig.26

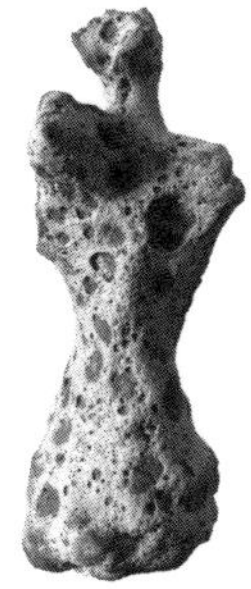

JH Daniel, these sculptures, as far as I know, haven't been shown before and they where chosen from the studio. To what extent are you conscious of what you want to achieve when you're making something? Or how intuitive? How do you tap into your unconscious when you are making a work?

DS I have a very, very small figurine on the desk in the study.

A few years ago I worked a lot with the body, but using mannequins, I hadn't ever really worked with a dancer or a model, so I started working with dancers in the studio. I'd invite them into a small office space at the back of my studio. I wanted to reverse the roles, so instead of me lying on the psychoanalytic sofa, they are now metaphorically lying on my sofa and I started a dialogue with them. I made clay figurines in different sizes which were not so much me modelling what they looked like, but was more about this relationship, this tapping into something that happens between the dancers and me and the ideas that come up. These actions are quite fast, they are very much about the hand and sometimes I don't even look at what I'm doing. It came from trying to move away from being in this world of words of analysis, they grew and grew in number, more and more of the clay figures. I would look back on what I had made and that would inform my next move so they became like a language.

Some of the clay figures were in my Frith Street Gallery show last year, in the original gallery space on Frith Street in Soho. I displayed the clay figures on tables with fabric. When it became possible to include one of them here, and Simon, that one that's on the table is really yours, for me it was like taking a dance now with Freud's sculpture collection. I know that I'm going to reuse that image over and over again, to contextualise what I do, with this embryonic figure dancing, or talking. It was a good surprise when I saw my figure on Freud's desk (pp.18–19) while installing the exhibition because a lot of times when you put a work in a different context, you don't know what to expect and when I came and I saw it, it was like, this is it. I was very happy. I have been working quite a lot with mannequins over the last few years, four or five years. I worked a lot previously with Greek sculptures as a reference and when people come to the studio and I explain Greek sculptures to them, I used to say that they where like modern day mannequins, they were painted pink, it was very much about the ideal body.

I used to work with mannequins so much, we copied them in the studio in marble. I wasn't happy with the bodies, so I just kept the heads. There's always this problem, when you make a head, where do you put it? so I put it on a mannequin. What was nice as well, is that Adele Rootsetein was a cousin of my grandma, so there was a family connection to this story. These small mannequin sculptures are based on a Roman bust from the Museum in Bath, that's why they are called *After Bath Mannequins* (pp.13, 24), and they use a textured marble for the bust and Onyx for the head.

SM I'm fascinated also by these works by Daniel because of the different elements of translation and the multiple layers of time and process present. The fact that he copies the mannequins in marble, initially carved in one way, then does some additional carving, sometimes defacing it so going against the original idea that he had copied. All of this I find really fascinating from the point of view of translation. Translation is another theme in the show, from conscious to unconscious, from idea to object, the role of translation in terms of the creative process of making an artwork. The idea of erosion, of carving away and removing layers I found really interesting and appropriate for the exhibition.

DS For me also in the historic clay objects in the study you could really feel the sense of the hand that's made them. They were made 2, 3, 4000 years ago, and you can really feel this humanity that is present in the touch and the movement in the clay. That's something which drives me, this idea of how things that we leave behind will be read in the future. If we can embody them with a sense of touch, that will be read in the future. It's especially relevant today when everything is so digital and doesn't allow that sense of humanity within it.

SM They are like a translations of your experience with the dancer in the moment.

JH Both of you very much play with classical and antique tropes but both of your work is, of course, extremely contemporary. There's an interesting parallel with Freud, an extremely modern thinker about how we travel through the world but who is obsessed with very, very old things. I think that's a really nice echo between Freud's interests and your interests.

SM That kind of sensibility also became another presence in the exhibition, I realised that I ended up selecting things which were figurative, a lot of them which were made in a very classical way like carving wood, carving marble, really timeless techniques. The classical references and even the figuration relates to also the heads, figures and busts in Freud's study.

JH When you're putting your collages together, the ones that you made for this show, what was your process?

SM Very much instinctive, very automatic, a fairly quick way of putting things together on the studio table. I put things together then look at it for a day or two, then I might decide to change something but in the end it has to feel very immediate and truthful somehow and not staged.

I am interested in the activity of collecting things and images, curating and choreographing and how we put things together, often in an automatic way. I am fascinated with the mechanism behind it in terms of desire and how it can be connected with memory, even very early memories, because often there are elements of the unconscious at play. Something from the past you're not consciously aware of, and this is possibly also why you are attracted to something. This is how I collect images in my studio because I don't organise them, I don't have neat boxes labelled flowers, rocks, seashells, etc. It's quite important for me that I forget the sources where the images come from so that everything gets mixed up in this other place, and then rescued and given a new context.

A few years ago I started to embrace a way of working with free association, I stopped pursuing the fantasy of an idea that I had in my head. I think sometimes artists work on this fantasy of an idea that

fig.27

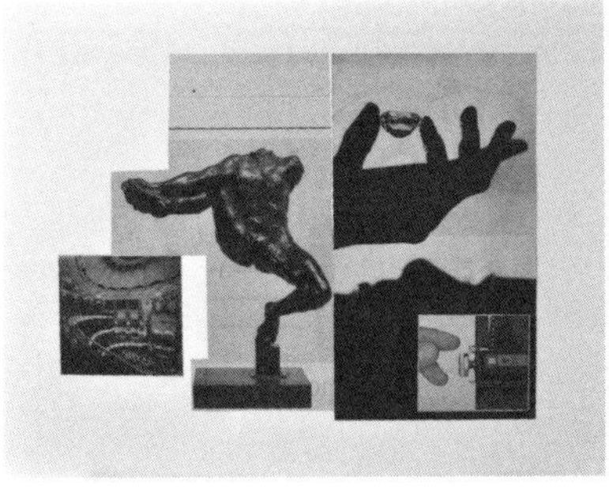

they try to translate and never get to it, sometimes it's an impossibility, this failure can be interesting and productive too and can take you somewhere else. But I started to work differently.

JH What about the world of dreams in your life?

DS There was a moment which happened to me once in analysis where I was lying on the couch in the analyst's room and the room felt huge, like when you're a child and you laying in bed, the ceilings seem much, much higher. I thought, is that a dream? or maybe that's more kind of a free association or reverie. I'm trying to recreate that now, I am taking those small figurines and making them very big, four metres high, so when we meet them we meet them more like a child. We don't try and analyse or compare them to the knowledge we have in our head, but just meet them in a kind of sculptural way, I think it's in a way recreating something which is like a dream.

Sometimes I have moments in the studio, which I have remembered or that I've maybe dreamed of in the past, but I have never woken up in the morning after a dream and said I'm going to make a piece now, that hasn't happened. I am trying to create those sweet moments of freedom that one can have in a dream allowing these moments of free association. Maybe I will try and build up a kind of family of objects that will allow that to happen.

JH How about in your work Simon?

SM I don't feel like there's an immediate connection with my dream world in terms of I had a dream and then I made something in the studio but certainly it's the same kind of language when we are talking about the unconscious and the things I was mentioning earlier.

JH The idea of time travel is very present in this house isn't it?

SM Yes, when I first came for a site visit the house was closed to the public. So there was nobody around which was great in a way because we could really look at everything. But it really made me feel like I wanted to imagine the family living here in the past. It's a personality museum so I immediately thought somehow I wanted to bring figures back, or to go back in time.

JH I also like the metaphor of the mirror and the mirrors you have included.

fig.28

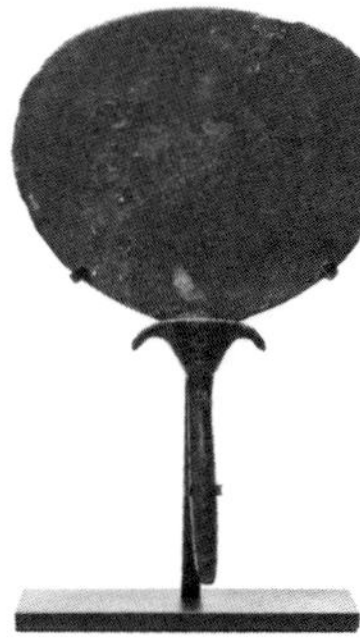

SM The ancient mirrors belonging to Freud have obviously been shown here before but they weren't on display recently, so I decided I really wanted to have them on show in conversation with my new print in the Hall (p.12) as it features a figure of a Minoan mirror holder. It was very exciting to thread a new narrative, a journey around the house, and a journey through time, and to make connections between our works, the archive of the journal, psychoanalytic ideas and of course the collection of the museum.

JH I've been wanting to say this in this house… I think our session is over.

fig.23 Giorgio de Chirico, *The Enigma of the Hour, (L'Énigme de l'heure)*, 1910/11, oil on canvas, 54.5 × 70.5 cm.
fig.24 Daniel Silver, installation view of *DIG*, 2013.
fig.25 Simon Moretti, *Untitled (Oedipus Rex-The Infernal Machine) #1*, 2019.
fig.26 Daniel Silver, *Moon Face*, 2018.
fig.27 Simon Moretti, *Untitled (NP 15)*, 2014, collage, 29.7 × 42 cm.
fig.28 Mirror, Egyptian, copper alloy, 1550–1069 BC. Museum no. 3325. Collection of the Freud Museum London.

Cover and inside cover
Selection of titles of papers published by *The International Journal of Psychoanalysis*

p.1
Original logo of *The International Journal of Psychoanalysis*, 1920s

p.2
Photograph of Freud's desk by psychoanalyst Heinz Weiss and archaeologist Carina Weiss, taken during a visit to 22 Maresfield Gardens, London, 1983

p.4, fig.1
Jean Auguste Dominique Ingres
Oedipus and The Sphinx, 1808
Oil on Canvas
189 × 144 cm
Musée du Louvre, Paris

pp.12–29
The Enigma of The Hour, installation view
Freud Museum London

p.13
Daniel Silver
After Bath Mannequins 1, 2018
Marble and Yellow Onyx, plinth
46 × 34 × 20 cm
Courtesy Frith Street Gallery

pp.16, 58
Linder
Inflora, 2013
Photomontage
19.1 × 16.5 cm
Courtesy the artist & Modern Art, London

p.17
Paloma Varga Weisz
Man, bent, 2019
Limewood, carpet
200 × 70 × 70 cm
Courtesy Sadie Coles HQ, London

p.19, fig.26
Daniel Silver
Moon Face, 2018
Glazed, fired clay
16 × 6 × 5 cm
Collection Simon Moretti

p.20, fig.6
Simon Moretti
Only Day and Night, 2019
Neon, cables, transformer, plexiglass
110 × 15 cm
Courtesy the artist
Commissioned by *The International Journal of Psychoanalysis*

p.21, fig.9
Goshka Macuga
International Institute of Intellectual Co-operation, Riviere, 2019
Rubber, resin
40 × 30 cm
Commissioned by *The International Journal of Psychoanalysis*

International Institute of Intellectual Co-operation, Freud, 2016
Concrete, Jesmonite
39 × 23 × 37 cm

International Institute of Intellectual Co-operation, Strachey, 2019
Rubber, resin
40 × 30 cm
Commissioned by *The International Journal of Psychoanalysis*
All courtesy the artist

p.22
Rodrigo Moynihan
Ernest Jones, 1946
Oil on canvas
97.4 × 84.7 cm
Collection of the British Psychoanalytical Society

p.23
The Enigma of The Hour, installation views (L to R: Linder, Duncan Grant, Paloma Varga Weisz, Goshka Macuga & Simon Moretti)
Freud Museum London

The Enigma of The Hour, installation views (Simon Moretti)
Freud Museum London

p.24, fig.13
Daniel Silver
After Bath Mannequins 2, 2018
Marble and Grey Onyx
46 × 34 × 20 cm
Courtesy Frith Street Gallery, London

p.26
Sergei Pankejeff
Painting of wolves sitting in a tree, 1965
Oil on canvas
45 × 55 × 3.5 cm
Museum no. 6464
Collection of the Freud Museum London

p.27, fig.11
Goshka Macuga
Somnambulist, 2006
Carved wood, fibreglass, hair, fabric clothes
33 × 200 × 53 cm
Courtesy Kate MacGarry, London

p.30
Photograph of Freud's library by psychoanalyst Heinz Weiss and archaeologist Carina Weiss, taken during a visit to 20 Maresfield Gardens, London, 1983

p.38
Linder
Post-mortem, Tatiana (i), 2016
Photomontage
26 × 21 cm
Courtesy the artist & Modern Art, London

Sergei Pankejeff
Painting of wolves sitting in a tree, 1965
Oil on canvas
45 × 55 × 3.5 cm
Museum no. 6464
Collection of the Freud Museum London

p.39, fig.12
Paloma Varga Weisz
Lazlo's dream, 2018
Limewood
Figure: 49.5 × 14.5 × 16.5 cm
Overall: 62.5 × 23 × 27 cm
Courtesy Sadie Coles HQ, London

p.40
Photograph of Freud's study by psychoanalyst Heinz Weiss and archaeologist Carina Weiss, during a visit to 20 Maresfield Gardens, London, 1983

p.41
Daniel Silver
Untitled 2014
Carrara marble, concrete
222 × 80 × 65 cm
Courtesy Frith Street
Gallery, London

p.42
Extract from *The Interpretation of Dreams* by Sigmund Freud, 1900. Translated by James Strachey, with assistance from Alix Strachey and Alan Tyson. Standard Edition 3-4: ix-627. Hogarth Press, and the Institute of Psycho-Analysis, London, 1952

p.43, fig.10
Barbara Ker-Seymer
and John Banting
Alix Strachey, 1930
27 × 19 cm
National Portrait Gallery, London
Courtesy of the Barbara
Ker-Seymer Estate

p.44
Linder
Lubov Tchemicheva, 2018
Photomontage
26 × 21 cm
Courtesy the artist &
Modern Art, London

p.45, fig.25
Simon Moretti
Untitled (Oedipus Rex-The Infernal Machine) #1, 2019
Screen print
95 × 76 cm each
Courtesy of the artist
Commissioned by *The International Journal of Psychoanalysis*

p.46
Goshka Macuga
Devil's Sonata, 2007
Etched mirror
91.44 × 152.4 cm
Courtesy of the artist and Andrew
Kreps Gallery, New York

Extract from *Introductory Lectures on Psycho-Analysis* by Sigmund Freud, 1916. Translated by James Strachey, with assistance from Alix Strachey and Alan Tyson. Standard Edition XV: 1-240. Hogarth Press and the Institute of Psycho-Analysis, London, 1933

p.47
Simon Moretti
Untitled (Oedipus Rex-The Infernal Machine) #2, 2019
Screen print
95 × 76 cm each
Courtesy of the artist
Commissioned by *The International Journal of Psychoanalysis*

p.48
Paloma Varga Weisz
Man, hanging, 2018
Limewood, hemp, rope
219 × 65 × 31 cm
Courtesy Sadie Coles HQ, London

Paloma Varga Weisz
Father, 2010
Glazed ceramic
23.0 × 21.0 × 20.0 cm
Courtesy Sadie Coles HQ, London

p.49
Linder
Post-mortem, Nobilissima Visione II, 2011
Photomontage
26 × 21 cm
Courtesy the artist &
Modern Art, London

p.50
Linder
Post-mortem, Symphonie Fantastique, 2011
Photomontage
26 × 21 cm
Courtesy the artist &
Modern Art, London

p.51, fig.7
Linder
Post-mortem, Alexandra (i), 2016
Photomontage
26 × 21 cm
Courtesy the artist &
Modern Art, London

p.52
Research photograph taken by Daniel Silver during a visit to the Freud Museum London, 2009

Goshka Macuga
International Institute of Intellectual Co-operation, Freud, 2016
Concrete, Jesmonite
39 × 23 × 37 cm
Courtesy of the artist and
Galerie Rüdiger Schöttle

p.53
Duncan Grant
James Strachey, 1910
Oil on canvas
64 × 76 cm
Tate

p.54
Extracts from *Dreamland and Somnambulism*, H.P.Blavatsky
From *A Modern Panarion*,
Vol.III No.4, January, 1882

p.55
Goshka Macuga as Cesare the somnambulist in the performance *The Cabinet of Dr Caligary*, Destino, London, 2004
Courtesy Paul Heber-Percy
& Simon Moretti

Goshka Macuga
Somnambulist, 2006
Carved wood, fibreglass, hair,
fabric clothes
33 × 200 × 53 cm
Courtesy Kate MacGarry, London

p.57
Simon Moretti
for Stuart Morgan, 2015-19
Screen print
100 × 76 cm
Courtesy the artist
Commissioned by *The International Journal of Psychoanalysis*

p.58
Linder
Inflora, 2013
Photomontage
19.1 × 16.5 cm
Courtesy the artist &
Modern Art, London

p.59
Photograph of Freud's study by psychoanalyst Heinz Weiss and archaeologist Carina Weiss,
taken during a visit to 20 Maresfield Gardens, London, 1983

p.60
Detail of cover showing the Sphinx from the film *Oedipus Rex* by Pier Paolo Pasolini 1967. From *Edipo Re*, Film e Discussioni, a cura di Giacomo Gamberti, Garzanti editore, 1967
Simon Moretti archive

p.61
Linder,
Lustron, 2013
Photomontage
19.9 × 15.3 cm
Courtesy the artist &
Modern Art, London

p.62
Extract from *Odedipus Rex*
The Theban Plays by Sophocles
Translated by E.F. Watling,
Penguin Classics, 1950

Paloma Varga Weisz
Mountaineer, 2014
Limewood
170.0 × 85.0 × 32.0 cm
Courtesy Sadie Coles HQ, London

p.63
Simon Moretti
Untitled (Stella Maris), 2012
Collage
42 × 30 cm
Courtesy the artist

p.64
Mirror, Bronze, Etruscan,
350-250BC. Museum no. 3082.
This mirror was a gift to Anna
Freud. It has a clear image of four
figures. Athena, goddess of war, is
on the right, armed with helmet,
spear and shield. We are not sure who
the other three figures are possibly
Helen of Troy, either being abducted
by Theseus, or taken by her
husband Menelaus.
Collection of the Freud
Museum London

p.65
Research photograph taken by Daniel
Silver during a visit to the Freud
Museum London 2009

p.66, fig.24
Daniel Silver
Installation view of *DIG*, 2013
The Odeon Site, 24 Grafton
Way. London, WC1
Commissioned by Artangel
Courtesy Frith Street
Gallery, London

p.67
Goshka Macuga
A History of Orgies, 2008
Fossilised wood, vintage
photograph, book
80 × 56 × 35 cm
Uziyel Collection, London
Courtesy of the artist and Kate
MacGarry, London

p.68
Goshka Macuga & Simon Moretti
Encounters in the Field, 2019
Screen print
95 × 76 cm
Courtesy the artists
Commissioned by *The International Journal of Psychoanalysis*

p.91
Research photograph taken by Daniel
Silver during a visit to the Freud
Museum London, 2009

Image Credits

Works of Art © the artists 2019
Items from the collection of
the Freud Museum, London
© Freud Museum, London
Items from the archive of *The International Journal of Psychoanalysis*
© The International Journal
of Psychoanalysis
Items from the British Psychoanalytical
Society: courtesy the Brtitish
Psychoanalytical Society

© Heinz and Carina Weiss: pp.2, 30,
40, 59, 96
© Scala / Art Resource, NY: p.4;
fig.23
© Angus Mill: pp.12-29, 58; fig.6, 9,
11, 13, 24
© Paloma Varga Weisz: pp.17, 39,
48, 62
© the Wellcome Collection, London
and the Melanie Klein Archive:
pp.24, 25, 80
Science History Images / Alamy
Stock: fig.16
Photo: Robert Glowacki: pp.39,
48; fig.12
© reserved; collection National
Portrait Gallery, London. Courtesy
of the Barbara. Ker-Seymer Estate.
Photo National Portrait Gallery,
London: pp.43, 79 (22); fig.10
© Pete Navey: pp.45, 47, 57, 68; fig.22
© Daniel Silver: pp.52, 65, 91
© Tate, London 2019: p.53
© Simon Moretti: p.55
Photographer unknown: p.60
© Alice May & Marcus Leith: p.66; fig.24
Wikimedia Commons: fig.19
© Andy Holmes: fig.20
Decla-Bioscop AG / Goldwyn Distr.
ScreenProd / Photononstop / Alamy
Stock: fig.21
Photo: Ardon Bar Hama: p.74 (2-4)
© The Estate of Barbara Ker-Seymer.
Photo National Portrait Gallery,
London: p.81

Great care has been taken to identify
all image copyright holders correctly.
In cases of errors or omissions please
contact the publisher so that we can
make corrections in future editions.

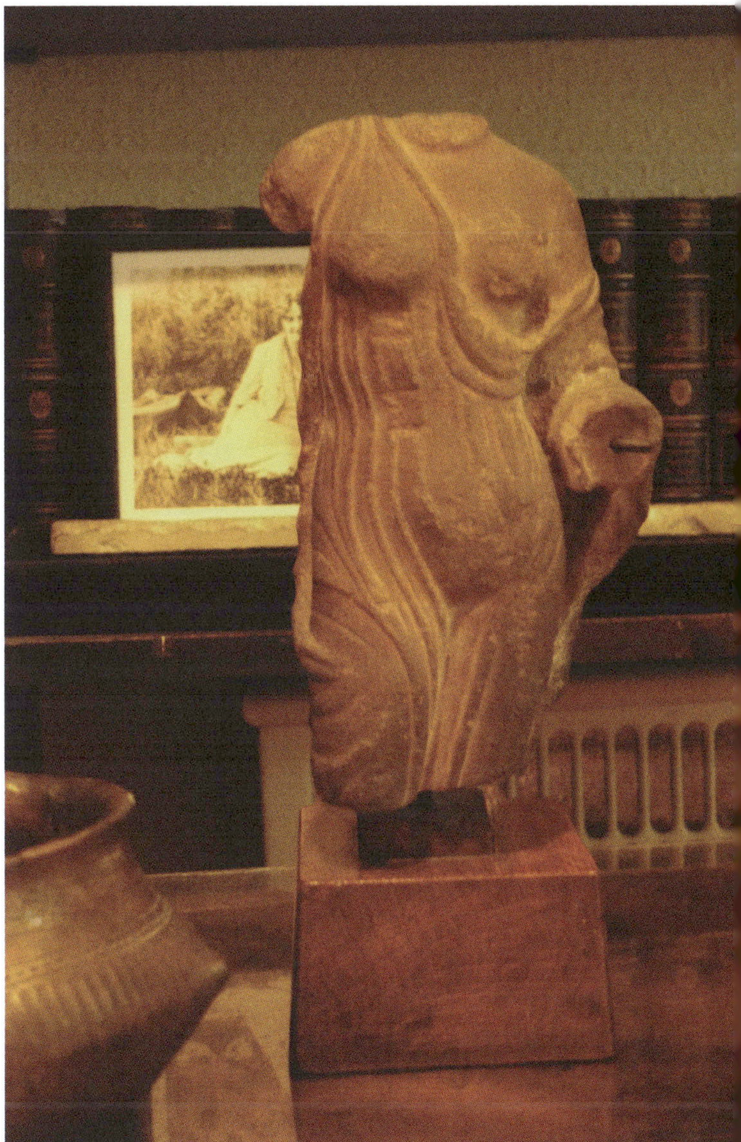

Jennifer Higgie (b.1962, Australia) is a writer and editorial director of *frieze* magazine. In 2017, her first children's book, *There's Not One*, was published by Scribe; she also is the editor of *The Artist's Joke* (MIT, 2007), the novel *Bedlam* (Sternberg Press, 2006) and is the screenwriter of the feature film *I Really Hate My Job* (2007). She is currently writing a book on female self-portraits titled *The Mirror and the Palette*. It will be published by Weidenfeld & Nicolson.

Linder (b.1954, UK) is a British artist known for her photography, radical feminist photomontage, and confrontational performance art. Emerging from the Manchester punk and post-punk scenes in the 1970s, Sterling focuses on questions of gender, commodity and display.

Exhibitions include: *The House of Fame*, Nottingham Contemporary, Nottingham (2018); *Bower of Bliss*, Glasgow Women's Library (2018); *Her Grace Land*, Chatsworth, Derbyshire (2018); *As Above, So Below, Portals, Visions, Spirits & Mystics*, IMMA, Dublin (2017); *Performing for the Camera*, Tate Modern, London (2016); *Femme/Object*, Musée d'Art Moderne de la Ville de Paris, Paris (2013).

Goshka Macuga (b.1966, Poland) moves beyond the traditionally perceived role of an artist creating installations in which she appropriates the work of other artists, archive material, ready-mades, but also objects of her own making using sculpture, drawing, photography and film. Macuga's working method is often referred to as cultural archaeology.

Exhibitions include: *Now this, is this the end... the end of the beginning or the beginning of the end?*, Schinkel Pavilion, Berlin (2016); *To the Son of Man Who Ate the Scroll*, Fondazione Prada, Milan (2016); *Accrochage*, Pinault Collection at Punta della Dogana, Venice (2016); *Time as Fabric*, New Museum, New York (2016); *dOCUMENTA (13)*, Kunsthalle Fridericianum, Kassel, DE and Queen's Palace, Kabul (2012).

Simon Moretti (b.1974, UK) is an artist and curator based in London. His work deals with context and display, through the use of appropriated images and archives, often collaborating with other artists. Moretti's recent work explores the idea of collage and speaks to traditions of collage and montage dating back to the nineteenth century, also often referencing art history, psychoanalytic and cultural theory.

Exhibitions include: *A Utopian Stage, to be free is to lose sight of the shore*, Dhaka Art Summit 18, Bangladesh (2018); *Revolt of the Sage*, Blain|Southern, London (2017); *The Camera Exposed*, Victoria & Albert Museum, London (2016); *Dadadandy Boutique*, Artprojx Space, London (2008); *The Art Parade*, Deitch Projects, New York (2007); *The Sleep of Ulro*, with Goshka Macuga, A Foundation, Liverpool Biennial, Liverpool (2006); *Thank You for the Music*, Sprueth Magers, London (2006); *None of the Above*, Swiss Institute, New York (2004).

Michael Newman (b.1954, UK) is a writer, art historian and critic. He has written books on Richard Prince, Jeff Wall and Seth Price, and co-edited *Rewriting Conceptual Art* (1999) and *The State of Art Criticism* (2007). He has published numerous essays on modern and contemporary artists, as well as thematic essays on the wound, the horizon, contingency, memory, the trace of drawing and nonsense. He has curated exhibitions at Independent Curators Inc, New York, the Fruitmarket Gallery, Edinburgh and ICA, London. He is currently Professor of Art Writing at Goldsmiths College in the University of London.

Daniel Silver (b.1972, UK) is best known for his figurative sculptures. His practice is deeply influenced by the art of ancient Greece, Modernist sculpture, and Freudian psychoanalytic theory. Silver's works use concrete, bronze, marble, stone, wood and clay, and often appear as monuments or totems, as if belonging to an archeological excavation.

Exhibitions include: The New Art Gallery Walsall (2019); Frith Street Gallery, London, UK (2018); ISelf Collection: *Bumped Bodies*, Whitechapel Gallery, London (2018); *Gestalt*, Hydra School Projects, Hydra (2017); *Rock Formations*, Art Basel Parcours, Antikenmuseum, Basel (2015); *Dig*, Artangel London (2013); *The Smoking Silver Father Figures*, Frieze Sculpture Park, London (2010); *Heads*, Camden Arts Centre, London (2007).

Adele Tutter (b.1961, USA) M.D. Ph.D. is Assistant Professor of Psychiatry, Columbia University Vagelos School of Medicine, and Faculty, Columbia University Center for Psychoanalytic Training and Research and the New York Psychoanalytic Institute. Author of numerous interdisciplinary articles, her monographs include *Dream House: An Intimate Portrait of the Philip Johnson Glass House* (author); *Grief and its Transcendence: Memory, Identity, Creativity* (co-editor, with Léon Wurmser); and *The Muse: Psychoanalytic Explorations of Creative Inspiration* (editor). She practices psychoanalysis in Manhattan.

Marina Warner (b.1946, UK) is a writer of fiction, criticism and history; her works include novels and short stories as well as studies of art, myths, symbols and fairytales.

Her critical and historical books and essays explore different figures in myth and fairy tale, such as the Virgin Mary, *Alone of All Her Sex: The Myth and the Cult of the Virgin Mary* (1976) and Joan of Arc, *Joan of Arc: The Image of Female Heroism* (1981); more recently she has written on fairy tales, *Stranger Magic: Charmed States & The Arabian Nights* (2011), and artists, *Forms of Enchantment: Writings on Art and Artists* (2018).

Paloma Varga Weisz (b.1967, Germany) is recognised by her diverse oeuvre which includes sculptures and installations mainly in wood and ceramics, as well as watercolours and drawings. Paloma Varga Weisz was originally trained as a wood carver in Garmisch-Partenkirchen. Her works embrace many of the aspects of style and subject matter of the arts and crafts of the Middle Ages, creating evocative works that recall folklore and as well as her layered personal iconography.

Exhibitions include: *Root of a Dream*, Castello di Rivoli, Italy (2016); Paloma Varga Weisz, Fürstenberg Zeitgenössisch, Donaueschingen (2016); *NO MAN'S LAND*: Women Artists from the Rubell Family Collection, Rubell Family Collection/Contemporary Arts Foundation, Miami (2015); *Krummer Hund*, Kabinett für aktuelle Kunst, Bremerhaven (2013).

The International Journal of Psychoanalysis was founded by Ernest Jones with the collaboration of Sigmund Freud in 1920. Today it's the première scholarly journal for psychoanalysis, with an international readership of over 8,000. Past editors have included Ernest Jones, James Strachey, Joseph Sandler, and David Tuckett.

Its content includes fully peer-reviewed papers on Psychoanalytic Theory and Technique, Child and Adolescent Psychoanalysis, Inter-disciplinary papers, Clinical Communications, Research, The Analyst at Work, Letters, History of Psychoanalysis, Education, Psychoanalytic Controversies, Book Reviews and Film Essays.

The Freud Museum was the final home of Sigmund Freud, the founder of psychoanalysis, and his daughter Anna Freud, a pioneering child psychoanalyst. The Freud family came to England as refugees, having escaped Austria following the Nazi annexation in March 1938. Freud spent the last year of his life there, and it remained the family home until Anna's death in 1982. It opened its doors to the public in 1986. The Freud Museum exists to promote the intellectual and cultural legacies of Sigmund and Anna Freud.

Acknowledgements

The editors would like to thank

The artists
Linder, Daniel Silver, Paloma Varga Weisz

The authors
Jennifer Higgie, Michael Newman, Adele Tutter, Marina Warner

Outset Contemporary Art Fund for supporting this publication
Candida Gertler, Marta Arenal, Isabel Sacks, Nina Montironi

Koenig Books, London
Franz König, Eva Möller

The International Journal of Psychoanalysis
Dana Birksted-Breen, Grainne Lucy

The Enigma of the Hour Exhibition Group
A group of psychoanalysts and researchers who have worked with the curators on the exhibition over the course of 15 months: Jan Abram, Rachel Blass, Georg Bruns, Christine Diercks, Lucy LaFarge, Dee McQuillan, Nellie Thompson, Francis Grier, Margot Waddell, Adele Tutter, Carina Weiss, Heinz Weiss, Ewan O'Neill

Freud Museum London
Bryony Davies, Francisco da Silva, Daniel Bento, Carol Siegel, Lili Spain, Stefan Marianski, Karolina Urbaniak

A Practice for Everyday Life

Frith Street Gallery, Andrew Kreps Gallery, Kate Macgarry, Galerie Rüdiger Schöttle, Modern Art, National Portrait Gallery London, Sadie Coles HQ, Tate

And would also like to thank
Jacob Bates-Firth, Craig Burnett, Andree Cooke, Eleanor Crabtree, Nicholas Cullinan, Rowan De Saulles, Stephen Grosz, Jessica Harrington, Mark Jenkins, Max Ker-Seymer, Ingrid Lohaus, Nicola Luckhurts, Lizzy Mason, Janet Marshall, Carolina Mazzolari, Dale McFarland, Sam Meredith, Angus Mill, Saven Morris, Danny Moynihan, Lisa Olrichs, Holly Peel, Ed Pennicott, Luke Perry, Fintan Rayan, Louie Rice, Isabel Sachs, Lieselotte Seaton, Freda & Izak Uziyel, Andrew Wilson

We would like to acknowledge the support of the British Psychoanalytical Society, European Psychoanalytical Federation, International Psychoanalytical Association, Robert Bosch Foundation, Sigmund-Freud Institut, Heidehof-Stiftung Foundation, Barbara Ker-Seymer Estate, Melanie Klein Archive, Outset Contemporary Art Fund, Wellcome Collection, Sadie Coles HQ, Freda & Izak Uziyel

outset.

Celebrating 100 1920-2019

FREUD MUSEUM LONDON

INTERNATIONAL PSYCHOANALYTICAL ASSOCIATION

Institute of Psychoanalysis British Psychoanalytical Society

Robert Bosch Stiftung

EPF FEP

SFI Sigmund-Freud Institut

Heidehof Stiftung

This catalogue is published on the occasion of the exhibition *The Enigma of the Hour: 100 years of Psychoanalytic Thought*, curated by Simon Moretti with Goshka Macuga and Dana Birksted-Breen at Freud Museum London, 6 June–4 August 2019.

Commissioned by
The International Journal of Psychoanalysis

© 2019 Simon Moretti & Goshka Macuga, authors and Koenig Books, London

All rights reserved. No part of this publication may be reproduced, stored in a retrieval system or transmitted in any form or by any means, electronic, mechanical, photocopying, recording or otherwise, without the prior permission of the publisher.

Editors: Simon Moretti and Goshka Macuga
Assisted by Paul Heber-Percy
Design: A Practice for Everyday Life, London
Print: Graphius, Belgium

First published by Koenig Books, London

Koenig Books Ltd
At the Serpentine Gallery
Kensington Gardens
London W2 3XA
www.koenigbooks.co.uk

Distribution

Germany, Austria, Switzerland / Europe
Buchhandlung Walther König
Ehrenstr. 4
D–50672 Köln
Tel: +49 (0) 221 / 20 59 6 53
verlag@buchhandlung-walther-koenig.de

UK & Ireland
Cornerhouse Publications Ltd.–HOME
2 Tony Wilson Place
UK–Manchester M15 4FN
Tel: +44 (0) 161 212 3466
publications@cornerhouse.org

Outside Europe
D.A.P. / Distributed Art Publishers, Inc.
75 Broad Street, Suite 630
USA - New York, NY 10004
Tel: +1 (0) 212 627 1999
orders@dapinc.com

ISBN 978-3-96098-698-0

Printed in Belgium

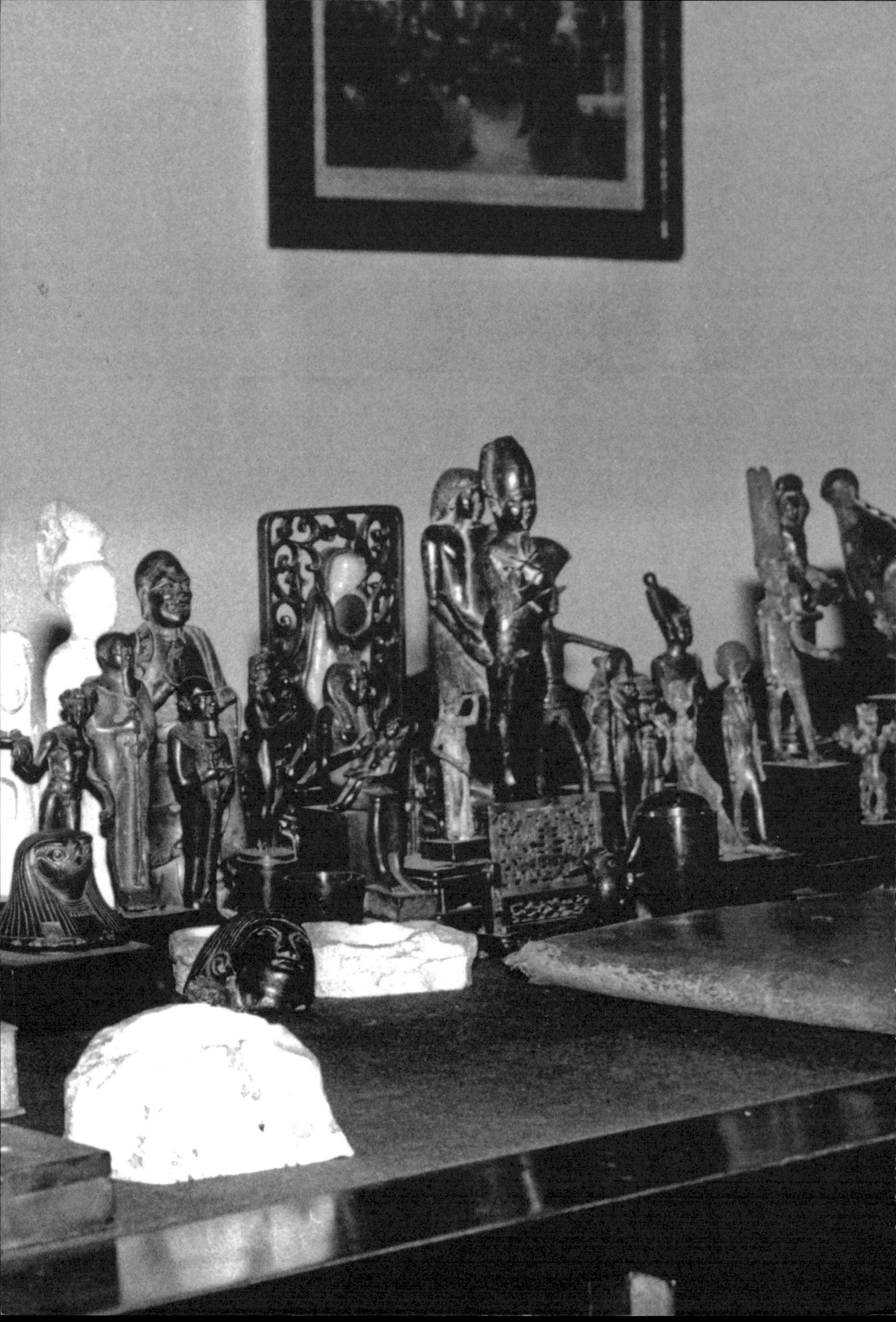